C000089224

DOLLS' HOUSES

THE
COLLECTOR'S
CORNER

DOLLS' HOUSES

Grange
BOOKS

CONTENTS

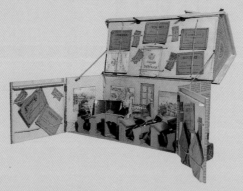

BELOW A small wooden dolls' house from Vyatka in Siberia which is now in a British collection. It may have been brought out of Russia during the revolution.

caused enormous social changes in the western world. The building of railways led to easier travel, haulage and communication, which led in turn to the rise of great manufacturing industries. A new, prosperous middle class was established whose needs were provided for by factory mass-production. From about 1830 more and more dolls' houses and other toys were manufactured in England, Europe and in the USA for the children of this emerging class.

In the middle of the nineteenth century the printing technique of lithography was invented. This development meant that manufacturers were able easily to decorate cheap wooden or cardboard houses, cutting costs still further.

These mass-produced dolls' houses cannot compare in terms of quality with the hand-crafted houses of the eighteenth century. The inferior, thin wood reclaimed from orange boxes or soap boxes which was often used to manufacture them has not lasted very well and the rooms tend to be badly proportioned, with little architectural detail.

Hand-made houses, however, still had facades and interiors as well constructed as those of the previous century and a great many dolls' houses from this period have survived. They may be in poor condition when you buy them, but repairing and restoring them is not difficult (though it can be time-consuming) and can be very enjoyable.

European roots

Old dolls' houses seem to have originated primarily from northern Europe where, due to the climate, life has always tended to be centred around the home. They are less usual in southern Europe, in spite of this area's tradition of making miniature Christmas Crêches, many of which contained detailed wooden figures to delight children (even if they were not allowed to play with them).

Mon plaisir

In the eighteenth century a wealthy German widow Princess Augusta Dorothea of Schwartzburg-Gotha created a fully populated dolls' town which she called 'Mon Plaisir'. It consists of over eighty rooms in glass-fronted boxes of many sizes and shapes. The whole life of a German eighteenth century town is portrayed in these boxes rather like a theatrical event, with realistic-looking dolls acting the parts of royal personages and ordinary citizens. To create this amazingly detailed miniature world, the Princess went deeply into debt as she paid for the materials and for her small army of craftworkers. This series of rooms can still be seen at the Castle Museum in Amstadt, Germany.

Mon Plaisir has a great many shops among its eighty or so cabinets illustrating eighteenth century life. They include a baker's shop, and an apothecary's shop, which is obviously based on the real thing, with its wooden counter and drawers and labelled bottles. The draper's

BELOW Two exquisitely dressed court ladies take tea in one of the rooms of Mon Plaisir.

shop depicts a fine lady looking at a roll of fabric. She is surrounded by a display of hats and bonnets, while in the background more fabrics are stacked in neat rolls. The tailor's shop shows the tailor sitting cross-legged, hard at work in his shop, with completed ladies' dresses hanging behind him on the walls. A court lady is ordering a dress from him. In other shops the joiner is at work on a set of chairs, the weaver is at his loom, the turner at his lathe and in the baker's shop the baker and his comely wife, holding a baby, offer a selection of bread and rolls.

Mon Plaisir also shows several market stalls set out in a complete street peopled by a wig seller, a supplier of cooking pots, a hat seller and a cloth seller. Down below in the same cabinet there is a woman selling vegetables, a rope seller and a shoe seller, all doing a brisk trade among their fellow citizens.

The Germans dominated the toy market for the whole of the nineteenth century, exporting vast numbers of dolls and toys, and quantities of dolls'-house furniture.

Early Dutch houses

The splendour of the houses which were produced in Holland throughout the eighteenth century has to be seen to be believed. In a similar style to the German houses, the Dutch dolls' houses were rooms set in cabinets, filled with fine miniature furniture, and household paraphernalia – made of glass, silver, porcelain and ivory. The rooms were often inhabited by little wax dolls dressed in silks and satins.

RIGHT Anne
Sharp's dolls'
house measures
1.75m (5ft 8in). It
is populated by a
family and their
servants, each of
whom has their
name written on
a piece of paper
pinned to their
clothing.

It is also a good idea to join a collectors' club through which you will meet fellow dolls' house enthusiasts who will undoubtedly be a valuable source of advice and information. You may also be able to swap furnishing odds and ends.

Read books and magazines on dolls' houses. It is well worth subscribing to the magazine *International dolls' House News*, which is full of the latest information about dolls' houses and miniature fairs, meetings of collectors, and suppliers of everything from knitting and sewing patterns for making your own dolls to bed linen for the miniature bedroom.

Old catalogues can also be a fascinating and useful source of reference. For example, in 1793, the German toy seller Georg Bestelmeier issued nine instalments of his catalogue of toys, each of which was fully described and illustrated with beautifully drawn copperplate engravings. These catalogues provide a rich mine of information about what was available during the late eighteenth and early nineteenth century, not only in Germany but in the rest of Europe to which the toys were exported.

Where to find dolls' houses

Dolls' houses can be found at antique fairs and in antique shops, auction rooms at specialist toy sales and even at car-boot sales.

RIGHT The sheer range of items that can be used to fill a dolls' house make collecting and furnishing dolls' houses an engrossing hobby.

ABOVE A miniature wooden shop from the Stadtmuseum, Munich. All the goods on display are modelled in wax.

wooden-headed doll stands behind her stall selling a variety of domestic utensils such as mops, shovels, brooms, and salt and knife boxes.

The Bethnal Green Museum of Childhood has an early market stall dated 1830, which they call a dolls' bazaar. The woman figure is selling haberdashery, including ribbons, reticules, pictures, packets of pins and a large doll. She is a close relative of the well known pedlar dolls so popular in Victorian days and seen in countless collections. Often the name of the pedlar and the date was written in ink on a piece of paper and pinned to the tray, just as the real-life pedlars of the time had to display their names on their licence-to-sell.

German production

Germans shops produced during the nineteenth century are delightfully imaginative and varied. There are millinery shops, with small dolls' heads showing off the bonnets and hats for sale; drapers' stores with cloth and drawers overflowing with buttons, ribbons and reels of thread; pottery shops with rows and rows of tiny jugs and bowls; flower shops; and dozens of others which are equally charming. The shapes of the miniature shops are as varied as the goods being sold; some look just like real shops with counters and shelves; others are in boxes with flaps that open out to reveal the goods inside.

Miniature market places with stalls were a speciality of southern Germany, and they were sold in boxed sets which could be built up by children, who could move from stall to stall buying what they wished. Others, such as the twentieth century copy of an earlier design from Erzgebirge in the toy museum at Sonneberg, had their goods stuck to the stalls, which made them less satisfactory as toys.

Some excellent examples of toy shops can be seen in the Toy Museum in Nuremberg. One is a millinery shop of about 1820, selling bonnets displayed on little papier mâché models, along with reticules, chemisettes, handkerchiefs, pictures with hooks to hold keys, and a mask to be worn at a ball. A sweet shop offers 'humbugs from Sweet Tooth and Co', 'London Peppermints' and jars full of jams and jellies. A basket shop dating from 1858 displays the wide range of handmade baskets that were available at the time and the variety of designs with which they were decorated. Some of the goods on show are hand-painted.

Grocery shops were also educational toys, teaching children how to trade, how to use money and give the right change. They could be very spectacular, one offering jars, packages, bottles and tins of labelled biscuits, sauces, tea, coffee, cheese, bread, fish and sweets, backed up by a formidable array of drawers containing dry goods labelled 'Anis', 'Nelken', 'Ilvanille', 'Niisse', 'Zimt', 'Nudeln', and so on. All these items were free-standing, so that a child could have a wonderful time taking them out and playing with them.

Fashion and millinery shops were particularly popular during the latter part of the nineteenth century, and they contained caps, veils, shawls, gowns with accessories, jabots, collars, cuffs, belts and stays, not to mention embroidered bell pulls, cushion covers, braces and suspenders, starched collars and shirt fronts for men. Everything had its rightful place on a shelf, a hanger or in a drawer.

BELOW A market scene made in Germany in the 1920s in the Sonneberg area.

of the John Wanamaker stores depicts a poultry shop with living quarters above. Several butcher's shops are shown in the Gamages catalogues from the early twentieth century.

More modern shops

The tradition of dolls' shops has continued into the twentieth century. A fine-quality milliner's shop in the Bethnal Green Museum of Childhood was produced in the 1920s. Many children growing up in the 1930s can recall the magic of their first sweet shop with its little glass jars of dolly mixtures and the grocer's shop.

Cecil Coleman Ltd of London advertised a Peter Pan Store for sixpence in 1933. It was a large folding shop. Printed in attractive colours and came complete with miniatures filled with sweets, scale, scoop, invoices and bags.

The firm of Tri-ang produced two shops in 1951: one with bright modern decor, complete with revolving door, counters and display shelves; another with an apartment above for the owner – all very modern.

That craft workers of today are well aware of the attraction of miniature shops is shown in the lovely toy shop made by the late Yootha Rose, and the antique shop by Joan Gibson, made in the 1980s.

The modern craftsman Frank Egerton also produces butchers' shops in which all the joints of meat can be detached from their hooks.

Dutch shops

A variation on the usual run of shops is seen in Holland, where in the Simon van Gijn museum there is an attractive Tabak, Snuif, Koffij, Thee shop in which these goods are displayed in large drums, as presumably they were in real life in the nineteenth century.

BELOW This English cardboard shop probably dates from about 1890.

Shops made of paper

Paper shops were being made in Germany in the mid-nineteenth century. In her book *Collecting dolls' houses and Miniatures*, Norah Earnshaw shows a folding paper dress shop, containing four paper dolls and a table with four bonnets on it. When not in use, the room folded into its box. By the end of the nineteenth century, brightly colored folding cardboard shops were sold with cut-out paper customers.

Miniature rooms

Miniature rooms were made in France and Germany as long ago as the seventeenth century. In 1607 Heroard, physician to the young Dauphin of France, recorded dolls' rooms from the early years of the seventeenth century, which belonged to the Dauphin's sisters.

The writer D'Allemagne describes how in 1675 a gilded room containing a four-poster bed was given to the Duc de Maine by Madame Thianges inscribed "Ta Chambre du Sublime".

Cardinal Richelieu presented the Princess d'Enghien with a model intended as a toy, which showed a mother lying in a bed surrounded by a nursemaid, midwife and grandmother. Reputedly, the young Princess was told that she was allowed dress and undress the dolls in this room, but that she could not bath the baby, because it was made of wax.

Learning through play

Shops and rooms were often used to teaching housewifely tasks. Miniature kitchens, were a popular gift to a girl as long ago as 1572, when the Princess of Saxony was given one. Toy kitchens were especially popular in Germany, where even middle-class girls were expected to be familiar with the work of the kitchen. Models kitchens in the Nuremberg tradition such as the one in the Metropolitan Museum of Art, New York were made well into the twentieth century. They give a fascinating insight into life of the period. Originally they were wood, with copper and pewter utensils, but gradually they became smaller in size and were made of tin.

Several toy kitchens can be seen in the toy museum, Nuremberg. One is a well equipped Franconian kitchen, dating from 1830 – with a metal utensils, a flat iron with a heating block inside, a drum for roasting coffee, an earthenware roasting pot and a stand for beer-mugs.

BELOW William Randolph Hearst, the American newspaper magnate owned this detailed kitchen, which includes irons, breadboards, a poacher, a roaster and a teakettle among its array of kitchen paraphernalia.

NOTABLE SEVENTEENTH AND EIGHTEENTH CENTURY HOUSES

● ● ● ●

The earliest dolls' house (or baby house as it would have been called then) still in existence is dated 1611. This heavy, wooden cabinet built in the shape of a house, 2.75 m (9 ft) high, 1.8m (6ft) wide and 0.6m (2ft) deep is in the Germanisches National Museum, Germany. The base of the house is the cellar, and the ground floor contains a Great Hall and a yard with a triple gallery, and a garden.

Stairs from the yard lead to the second floor, where there is a delightful kitchen containing a vast array of utensils and a living room, which was modernized in the eighteenth century. A bedroom on the top floor contains a huge bed, and a stateroom.

The Stromer house

The 1639 house known as the Stromer house, can be seen in the Germanisches National Museum. The house was named after the last owner, Baron von Stromer. At a little under 2.1m (7ft) high, it is slightly smaller than the

1611 house, and it contains over a thousand objects which provide a unique picture of domestic life in a prosperous seventeenth century German household.

RIGHT Dated 1611, this is the earliest known dolls' house still in existence. It has two halls, five rooms and a cellar and garden. This 2.75m (9ft) tall dolls' house can be seen at the Germanisches Nationalmuseum, Germany.

KING'S LYNN BABY HOUSE

The King's Lynn baby house (made in about 1740) was found with only its original panelling, door and fireplaces, but perhaps what it lacks in furniture is made up for by its interesting history. It is a replica in miniature of 27 King Street, King's Lynn, Norfolk, England once the home of a Dutch merchant named Flierden and his wife, who had the baby house built for their child, Ann.

In the 1920s a local dignitary gave the baby house to a Torquay children's home run by the Children's Society. Before that it had been kept somewhere in Bath. The house was restored in 1984 by Vivien Greene and a group of craftswomen who furnished the two bedrooms, dining room, music room, kitchen and counting house with modern furniture in a style suitable to the period and in accord with the Flierdens' Quaker beliefs. More recently the house has been on display at Powderham Castle, near Exeter, in Devon.

ABOVE. The counting house in the King's Lynn baby house was furnished simply because the merchant was a Quaker.

LEFT. The King's Lynn baby house was modelled on number 27 King Street, King's Lynn England.

RIGHT. The King's Lynn baby house had only its original panelling, door and fireplaces when it was rescued.

THE UPPARK BABY HOUSE

A huge eighteenth century masterpiece is housed at Uppark, in England. Uppark itself was partially destroyed by fire in 1989, but the elegant dolls' house which was brought to her new home by Sarah Lethieullier when she went there as the bride of Sir Matthew Fetherstonhaugh in 1747, was fortunately saved for posterity.

The baby house has been left untouched, so its beautiful Queen Anne exterior and its nine rooms on three floors, each room opening separately, are a perfect time-capsule of life in a great country house some 250 years ago. There are delicate architectural details such as brass doorlocks and knobs, panelled walls and marble fireplaces with brass fire-grates. The furnishings are simple and graceful and probably date a little earlier than the baby house.

The inhabitants of the house conform to the early-eighteenth century convention that servants were made with wooden heads while the gentry were made of wax and dressed in fine clothes. Each lady wears the correct cap and gown, and even the right number of petticoats; the gentleman of the house wears fashionable clothes and a powdered wig, and he carries a sword at his side, as was the custom for men at this time. The family is seated in the parlour taking tea and the dining room table, attended by liveried footmen, is laid for a meal with silver table settings under a silver chandelier.

As in the Dutch baby houses, there is a lying-in room, occupied by a mother and nurse, and dotted about the house are miniature paintings, some of which may have been painted by Lady Sarah herself, for she was an accomplished artist.

LEFT A portrait of Sarah Lethieullier who brought her baby house to Uppark, England during the 18th century.

BELOW The Uppark house is a beautifully furnished, large structure containing nine rooms on three floors.

by his architect James Paine, who based it on the real Nostell Priory. The rooms have carved panelling and mouldings, each fender is separately designed. The period furniture is said to have been made by the famous furniture maker Thomas Chippendale, and the rooms were decorated by Lady Winn and her sister. The small parlour is decorated with Chinese wallpaper.

The Tare baby house

The Tare baby house, dated 1760 (named after its donor, Mrs Walter Tare), is in the Bethnal Green Museum of Childhood. The exterior has an accurate facade and double staircase leading to a pedimented front door. Four rooms are visible through the windows – a bedroom, dining room and two reception rooms.

There is also a kitchen in the basement which can only be seen when the sections of the house are separated. The house was modernized and updated in 1830.

The house at Strangers' Hall

Strangers' Hall in Norwich has a solid wooden house with carrying handles, dated about 1720. The outside of the house is painted to look like brickwork, and it is clearly a toy that has been played with by children.

The Yarburgh baby house

The Castle Museum in York has the Yarburgh baby house, dated about 1751 and made for the children of the Heslington family. It consists of nine rooms, each opening independently.

RIGHT The well-equipped kitchen in the 18th century dolls' house at Stranger's Hall, England. The hastener on the left of the fireplace was used for cooking meat.

Germany

Germany in the nineteenth century was noted more for the quality and variety of the dolls'-house furniture, produced there and exported around the world, than for the dolls' houses themselves. However there were some manufacturers of note.

Christian Hacker and Co

A famous German manufacturer named Christian Hacker, who was working towards the end of the nineteenth century and early twentieth, specialized in attractive French-looking houses with mansard roofs, some with a central staircase. It was a style of dolls' house which was to remain popular until the 1930s.

Christian Hacker and Co was a firm of toymakers founded in Nuremburg in 1870. Their trademark, registered in 1875, was a distinctive one of the intertwined initials 'CH' with a little crown on top.

This firm had a great influence on the design of later nineteenth century Continental houses. Indeed variations on the Christian Hacker style appeared for many years. A characteristic feature of the style is the line decoration on the cream-painted furniture. It is particularly noticeable in the kitchens, where it is often applied to dressers and fireplaces.

Some of the Christian Hacker houses open out on one side to reveal four rooms, hall and staircase, others open in two sections with a roof that lifts off and instead

ABOVE The kitchen of a dolls' house made by the Nuremberg toy maker Christian Hacker c1900.

The Victorian era

Perhaps the most popular concept of an ideal dolls' house is an elaborate Victorian plaything. The Victorian period lasted over 60 years Queen Victoria reigned in England from 1837 until 1901. Popular taste altered frequently and the era combined some new concepts with traditional designs, reshaping them into novel forms which became known as 'Victorian'.

of a staircase there is an extra room. In addition the facades of the houses vary too; some of them have balconies, others pillars.

A contemporary girls' magazine tells us that Christian Hacker did market research in England when he was exploring the English market, and he copied houses in London, but the most well known style is French.

BELOW A fine dolls' house c1880 from the Musée des Arts Décoratifs, Paris, with a typical mansard roof.

The French style

There is a house in the Musée des Arts et Traditions Populaires in Paris, which is furnished in typically French style, full of elegant silk hangings and white and gold furniture. The exterior is very like the Christian Hacker house, with its mansard roof and central balcony but it stands in its own balustraded garden and the front is decorated with orange lozenges.

Another typically French style of house, known as the Deauville house, began to appear towards the end of the nineteenth century. Deauville houses are small, rather like seaside boarding houses, with bay windows and steps up to the front door. They usually stand on a base which is painted to look like rock. The villas have two rooms and lithographed bricks and wallpaper.

Denmark

Copenhagen boasts several dolls' houses which can be seen in Legoland and in the Dansk Folkemuseum, which has more than twenty. Among these is the Villa Olga, a tall, narrow building in Danish Renaissance style, with ten windows in the front. There are four floors, the top and bottom floors opening separately, the middle two floors opening together. The bottom floor contains two storerooms, on the ground floor is a kitchen, on the third a salon, and on the top is a bedroom. The maids' rooms would have been in the attics.

house containing six rooms furnished in Swedish Victorian style, with a family of dolls all warmly wrapped up against the cold. Some of the furniture is German.

Finland

The Museovirasto in Helsinki, Finland, has several dolls' houses, the earliest of which, dated 1830, is a mixture of styles and sizes, and the Aina Friedman house, which was made for a merchant's daughter of that name in about 1860. The furniture was either home-made or imported from Germany, as the manufacture of dolls'-house furniture did not begin in Finland until late in the nineteenth century.

Switzerland

Switzerland has several nineteenth century houses, in the Historisches Museum, Basel. The most famous is the five-storey house made in 1850 by the Basel artist Ludwig Adam Kelterborn for his three daughters. This detailed cabinet house can be viewed from both sides. It has an attic, a laundry and a storage room on the ground floor, six other rooms and cellars, as well as a large central staircase with doors leading onto two balcony rooms. The windows at the sides of the building ensure that this house is well lit and the effect is one of well ordered, Swiss domesticity.

ABOVE This Swedish dolls' house is dated around 1856. It was arranged by Mrs Emily Kihlberg for her 13 children.

Sweden

Dolls' houses were also popular in Scandinavian countries in the nineteenth century. Some were locally made, while others were imported from Germany. The Nordiska Museet in Stockholm has the Emily Kihlberg

DRAWING ROOM

Tables of various sizes and styles were used in the drawing room throughout the period. They were often quite elaborate and expensive and were usually decorated with vases of flowers or other ornaments. An ornate fireplace would dominate the room, and a large mirror often hung above it. The walls would be hung with the householder's best pictures.

LEFT The drawing room was the place where musical entertainment would take place in the evening, often with the whole family joining in.

RIGHT An ornate, marble topped 'D' table adorned with a collection of Russian lacquer boxes.

The drawing room was traditionally the room to which the ladies withdrew after dinner, leaving the men at the dining table. It would be furnished in a feminine style. The drawing room was usually the largest in the house with a large window. it was the main entertaining and and reception room and the furniture would be comfortable and costly. It would often be crammed with furniture, partly to offer plenty of seating and partly as a form of display.

LEFT Oriental artefacts such as this cloisonné vase were very fashionable items of drawing room furniture.

RIGHT This exquisite Victorian parlour can be seen at the Toy and Miniature Museum of Kansas City.

CONSERVATORY

The conservatory reached the height of its popularity at the end of the nineteenth century. It often led off a study or library. It would usually have a tiled floor and stained glass, panelled walls. Furniture was usually bamboo or wicker, with cast iron urns or wrought-iron garden seats.

Potted palms, tropical plants and exotic birds in cages created an atmosphere of relaxation. The conservatory provided the perfect place for the nineteenth century householder to indulge in the fashionable pastime of cultivating plants and flowers.

LEFT A miniature resin replica of a cast iron garden bench.

RIGHT An elaborate miniature glass house made with real glass. Conservatories were more usually attached to the house.

LEFT The conservatory was a relaxing place to take tea among exotic palms and plants in pots.

BEDROOM

The bedroom was a private room and the look would be individual and personal. Light colours were often favoured. After 1840 matching furniture suites became fashionable, comprising the bed, armoire, dressing bureau, commode and washstand. Beds were often highly decorated. There might also be a writing des,k, chairs, footstools, an ottoman, shelves, a mirror and a chaise longue.

RIGHT The master bedroom would usually hold one or two comfortably padded, decorative chairs.

BELOW A bed in the Victorian Renaissance revival style. The sheets and pillows are real English linen trimmed with lace. The green coverlet is pure silk.

RIGHT Before indoor plumbing every bedroom would have a washstand which held a pitcher and bowl. This corner stand also has a matching chamber pot.

BELOW A view of the bay window of a Victorian bedroom in a miniature Italianate villa in San Francisco from about 1882.

BATHROOM

With the advent of indoor plumbing in the last quarter of the nineteenth century, washstands in the bedroom could be given taps and permanently fixed bowls with plug holes and piping for the waste water. Bathtubs were also given a permanent fixed site. Early bathrooms were often converted from dressing-rooms or small bedrooms and were usually quite large. Bedroom furniture, such as dressers, side tables and even sofas followed the washstand into the new room.

Early fixtures were boxed in cabinets to disguise their real function. By 1880 water closets were part of the bathroom furniture, but they were often in a separate cubicle.

LEFT Water closets were often located on their own at the rear of the house.

ABOVE An earlier style of bathtub set in a panelled wooden cabinet.

ABOVE The first water closets in Victorian bathrooms were boxed in wooden cabinets to disguise their real function.

BELOW A ceramic bidet bowl.

RIGHT A gas powered water heater with enamel and brass fitting, for use in a Victorian bathroom.

KITCHEN

The kitchen was essentially a place of work. Plain off-white walls and a scrubbed floor were the norm. This was the domain of the servants so ornamentation was usually at a minimum. There would be a scullery for household chores, and pantries for storing china, equipment and foods.

By the 1870s, particularly in America, more consideration was given to the people who worked in the kitchen. Ease of cleanliness, efficiency and a cheerfulness became more important factors. Rag rugs, carpet pieces or decorated oilcloths might be used to soften the appearance.

Wooden ice boxes became increasingly popular. There would be a large central table and a plumbed in sink. Essential items included: pastry board, rolling pin, grinding machine, scales, iron or copper pots, kettle, knives and choppers.

ABOVE The kitchen would be fitted out with a range of pots and pans, such as the cast iron set above, and other equipment to help the housewife.

LEFT A bright, clean looking American kitchen from after the Civil War. Decoration was kept to a minimum.

RIGHT A small labelled spice cabinet, designed to be hung on the wall.

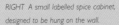

THE COLLECTOR'S CORNER

DOLLS' HOUSES

The Upper Hall

THE COLLECTOR'S CORNER

DOLLS' HOUSES

Grange
BOOKS

A Quantum Book

Published by Grange Books
an imprint of Grange Books Plc
The Grange
Kingsnorth Industrial Estate
Hoo, nr Rochester
Kent ME3 9ND

Copyright © 1999 Quantum Books Ltd

All rights reserved.
This book is protected by copyright. No part of it may be reproduced, stored in a retrieval
system, or transmitted in any form or by any means, without the prior permission in
writing of the Publisher, nor be otherwise circulated in any form of binding or cover other
than that in which it is published and without a similar condition including
this condition being imposed on the subsequent publisher.

ISBN 1-84013-295-7

This book is produced by
Quantum Books Ltd
6 Blundell Street
London N7 9BH

Project Manager: Rebecca Kingsley
Art Director: Siân Keogh
Project Editor: Jo Wells
Designer: Martin Laurie
Editor: Jo Wells

The material in this publication previously appeared in *Victorian Doll's Houses* and *Dollhouses*

QUMCCDH
Set in Gill Sans
Reproduced in Singapore by Eray Scan Pte Ltd
Printed in Singapore by Star Standard Industries (Pte) Ltd

CONTENTS

THE ORIGINS AND HISTORY OF MINIATURE HOUSES

● ● ● ●

Dolls' houses tell the story of how we arrange our domestic lives and through them we can glimpse the social customs and the objects that interested people of another age. We are fortunate that so many have survived the years in museums and in private collections to add their testimony to our knowledge of how our ancestors lived.

RIGHT AND OPPOSITE
A collector, Mrs Mollie Fox, was lucky enough to buy this late 18th-century dolls' house in the early 1970s. The house is gradually being restored in the style and colours of its period.

Although some of the more famous examples are large and elaborate, the charm of a dolls' house has little to do with such ostentation. Beautifully made tiny furniture and ornaments made of glass, wood or porcelain are as satisfying as those made from precious materials, for it is the three-dimensional picture of the world presented in miniature that charms us. Certainly children get just as much pleasure from playing with home-made chairs and tables made out of matchboxes as they do from craftsman-made objects purchased at great cost.

There is a wide choice of dolls' houses to buy. For those who prefer them, modern mass-produced houses are well made and reasonably priced. Skilled amateurs make their own dolls' houses, and this is a satisfying way of forming a collection; or, if you are rich enough, you can buy one of the many fine houses being created by enthusiasts today.

It is good to know that this great variety of dolls' houses will be passed on to future generations, to tell them the tale of how we ourselves once lived. Collecting dolls' houses encompasses a wide range of interests – from

RIGHT Dated
1639, the Stromer
house is one of
the earliest known
dolls' houses. It
stands over 2m
(6ft) tall and holds
six main rooms as
well as eight
workrooms and
servants rooms in
the base.

architecture and interior design to social history and modelling. For four centuries men and women have been captivated by dolls' houses, sometimes spending fortunes on the creation of their worlds in miniature. But great wealth is not necessary to become a collector. Although very old dolls' houses are expensive, more recent ones are not. However, you will need plenty of space and time for this hobby.

Ancient dolls' houses

We know that dolls' houses existed before the seventeenth century from the various clay, bronze and wooden items which have survived from Egyptian and Greek civilizations and which are now in museums throughout the world. Such models were not necessarily intended for children; many were funerary offerings and it is not until the fifteenth century, when northern European civilizations became more stable, that artists and craftsmen turned their attention to making secular miniatures as an extra form of income, creating little silver objects and miniature houses to put them in.

*I*f you find a doll's house in an out-of-the-way place, you will need transport to get it home and, as they can be quite heavy, a strong companion would also be useful.

Miniature houses from before the nineteenth century tended to be made for adult entertainment or occasionally as extravagant gifts for the children of the gentry. They were hand-crafted and very expensive.

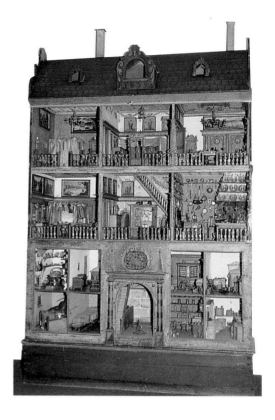

Because of their rarity and quality, dolls' houses from this period tend to be very expensive,

Duke Albrecht of Bavaria's fine dolls' house, created between 1557 and 1558 was an elaborate four-storey building set in a yard with a fountain and a garden with a silver well, a stable, cow shed, dairy and other domestic offices. In the house there was a bathroom, a dressing-room, and a kitchen. On the third floor was a ballroom, a bedroom and a withdrawing-room, and on the top floor was a chapel, another kitchen, nurseries, a sewing room and a bedroom. All the rooms were sumptuously furnished containing silver and tapestries. Sadly, this house was destroyed by fire in 1674.

Nineteenth century dolls' houses

Although craftsman-made dolls' houses were still being produced in northern Europe well into the eighteenth century, the Victorian age was characterized by the mass manufacture of inexpensive dolls' houses designed as playthings for children. These often had elaborate facades but poorly made interiors, lacking a staircase or doors to the rooms. Such houses were almost part of the furnishings of the English Victorian nursery and can be seen to this day in stately homes and museums throughout the country. The Victorian mass-produced dolls' houses also offer opportunities for the collector, for they do appear from time to time in antique shops and in auction sales.

Dolls' houses which had originally been adult toys became playthings for children in the nineteenth century. This shift happened for two main reasons. There had been a change of attitude towards children. In the early eighteenth century they were usually keep out of the way until they could behave like adults; but by the nineteenth

century, parents were on more intimate terms with their young and much more concerned about their education and upbringing than they had been in the past. The work of pioneer educationalists such as Locke, Rousseau and the Edgeworths was at last bearing fruit. It was understood that children could learn from their playthings, educational toys arrived in the nursery and among them were dolls' houses.

The second reason was that the industrial revolution, already begun in the previous century, had

BELOW An unpainted 18th century travelling dolls' house, which would probably have been used to entertain the children when parents visited friends.

BELOW A small
wooden dolls'
house from Vyatka
in Siberia which is
now in a British
collection. It may
have been brought
out of Russia
during the
revolution.

caused enormous social changes in the western world. The building of railways led to easier travel, haulage and communication, which led in turn to the rise of great manufacturing industries. A new, prosperous middle class was established whose needs were provided for by factory mass-production. From about 1830 more and more dolls' houses and other toys were manufactured in England, Europe and in the USA for the children of this emerging class.

In the middle of the nineteenth century the printing technique of lithography was invented. This development meant that manufacturers were able easily to decorate cheap wooden or cardboard houses, cutting costs still further.

These mass-produced dolls' houses cannot compare in terms of quality with the hand-crafted houses of the eighteenth century. The inferior, thin wood reclaimed from orange boxes or soap boxes which was often used to manufacture them has not lasted very well and the rooms tend to be badly proportioned, with little architectural detail.

Hand-made houses, however, still had facades and interiors as well constructed as those of the previous century and a great many dolls' houses from this period have survived. They may be in poor condition when you buy them, but repairing and restoring them is not difficult (though it can be time-consuming) and can be very enjoyable.

European roots

Old dolls' houses seem to have originated primarily from northern Europe where, due to the climate, life has always tended to be centred around the home. They are less usual in southern Europe, in spite of this area's tradition of making miniature Christmas Crêches, many of which contained detailed wooden figures to delight children (even if they were not allowed to play with them).

Dolls' houses were produced in greater numbers in Protestant countries and dolls' houses seem to share the same regional background as early traditions of the Christmas tree. They also proliferated in countries where modern ideas about child-care first evolved.

Dolls' houses have fascinated both adults and children for centuries, often inciting adults to wild extravagance as they indulged their passion for the miniature.

Early German dolls' houses

As long ago as the sixteenth century, Duke Albrecht of Bavaria had made a miniature replica of the house of a German prince, ostensibly for his small daughter, though when it was finally finished he placed it in a museum out of reach of childish fingers.

Duke Albrecht's dolls' house was destroyed by fire in 1674, but other examples of rich German merchants' houses of the seventeenth and eighteenth centuries can still be seen in the Germanisches National Museum, Nuremburg, Germany.

These very detailed miniature houses were filled with all the paraphernalia needed for comfortable living at that time and they were intended to teach young girls how to manage a household. They were known as 'baby houses' ('baby' being the word for a doll) until the late eighteenth and early nineteenth centuries. These baby houses, however, were not considered to be children's playthings, but were expensive and sophisticated adult toys.

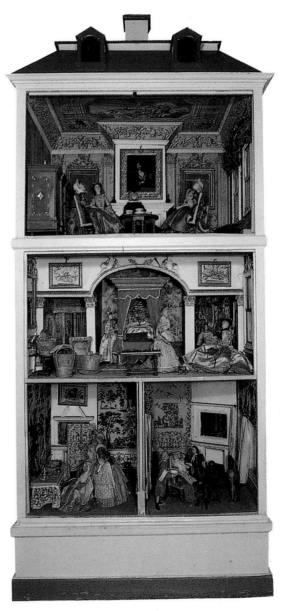

LEFT *The exterior of one of the Mon Plaisir houses with a well-to-do family and their servants going about their daily business.*

Mon plaisir

In the eighteenth century a wealthy German widow Princess Augusta Dorothea of Schwartzburg-Gotha created a fully populated dolls' town which she called 'Mon Plaisir'. It consists of over eighty rooms in glass-fronted boxes of many sizes and shapes. The whole life of a German eighteenth century town is portrayed in these boxes rather like a theatrical event, with realistic-looking dolls acting the parts of royal personages and ordinary citizens. To create this amazingly detailed miniature world, the Princess went deeply into debt as she paid for the materials and for her small army of craftworkers. This series of rooms can still be seen at the Castle Museum in Amstadt, Germany.

Mon Plaisir has a great many shops among its eighty or so cabinets illustrating eighteenth century life. They include a baker's shop, and an apothecary's shop, which is obviously based on the real thing, with its wooden counter and drawers and labelled bottles. The draper's

BELOW Two exquisitely dressed court ladies take tea in one of the rooms of Mon Plaisir.

shop depicts a fine lady looking at a roll of fabric. She is surrounded by a display of hats and bonnets, while in the background more fabrics are stacked in neat rolls. The tailor's shop shows the tailor sitting cross-legged, hard at work in his shop, with completed ladies' dresses hanging behind him on the walls. A court lady is ordering a dress from him. In other shops the joiner is at work on a set of chairs, the weaver is at his loom, the turner at his lathe and in the baker's shop the baker and his comely wife, holding a baby, offer a selection of bread and rolls.

Mon Plaisir also shows several market stalls set out in a complete street peopled by a wig seller, a supplier of cooking pots, a hat seller and a cloth seller. Down below in the same cabinet there is a woman selling vegetables, a rope seller and a shoe seller, all doing a brisk trade among their fellow citizens.

The Germans dominated the toy market for the whole of the nineteenth century, exporting vast numbers of dolls and toys, and quantities of dolls'-house furniture.

Early Dutch houses

The splendour of the houses which were produced in Holland throughout the eighteenth century has to be seen to be believed. In a similar style to the German houses, the Dutch dolls' houses were rooms set in cabinets, filled with fine miniature furniture, and household paraphernalia – made of glass, silver, porcelain and ivory. The rooms were often inhabited by little wax dolls dressed in silks and satins.

Ann Sharp's house is particularly interesting because it was a child's plaything, filled with simple furniture, not a costly adult toy. The house has been preserved, more or less as Ann left it, by the Bulwer Long family of Norfolk, It is often lent for display to museums and exhibitions.

Other English dolls' houses of the eighteenth century can be seen in England at Nostell Priory and at Uppark in England, (where a rare example was miraculously saved from fire), in the Museum of London, in the Bethnal Green Museum of Childhood, and in Vivien Greene's dolls' house collection at the Rotunda, Oxford.

LEFT AND BELOW Outdoor views were meticulously painted on the windows of the garden room in the 18th century van Amstel house. Each room in this elegant cabinet house was beautifully detailed and most contain sophisticated inhabitants.

These exquisite miniatures were intended neither as playthings for children nor as teaching aids for young women, but were the expensive hobby of wealthy merchants' wives with time on their hands who enjoyed recreating in detail the sort of houses in which they and their friends lived. These beautiful Dutch dolls' houses can be seen in museums in Amsterdam, The Hague, Haarlem and Utrecht.

Early English dolls' houses

In England at the beginning of the eighteenth century, Queen Anne presented her god-daughter, Ann Sharp, with a dolls' cabinet. This dolls' house still exists and is the earliest-known English dolls' house, except for an simple unpainted wooden, unfurnished baby house dated around 1675, which was sold at Sotheby's in London in 1988.

RIGHT Anne
Sharp's dolls'
house measures
1.75m (5ft 8in). It
is populated by a
family and their
servants, each of
whom has their
name written on
a piece of paper
pinned to their
clothing.

Scandinavian dolls' houses

There were also some early cabinet dolls' houses made in Sweden and Finland, and by the middle of the eighteenth century, dolls' houses were being made in the United States. The famous Van Cortland house, which was made in 1744, can be seen in the museum of that name in New York.

Early American dolls' houses

In America, dolls' houses were not mass-produced during the first part of the nineteenth century, but many beautiful early handmade examples exist in museums in different parts of the country.

Later in the century, American manufacturers such as McLaughlan, Schoenhut and Bliss dominated the dolls' house market. They began exporting their small cardboard and litho-printed wooden houses and bungalows to Europe, where they fitted comfortably into the smaller houses and apartments in which people were living towards the end of the century. These dolls' houses are also sometimes offered for sale, and are quickly snapped up by keen collectors.

LEFT A folding card dolls' house manufactured by the American firm McLaughlan in the late 19th century.

reproduction furniture from shops and markets quite easily. It is also quite easy to make some quite convincing items for yourself, by referring to books about furniture of the period and copying original designs. The basic tools that you will need to fashion your own furniture are: a sharp craft knife and glue. The basic materials can range from balsa wood, matchboxes, cardboard to easily found scraps of fabric.

Furniture

If you decide to use only authentic period furniture, then furnishing an old dolls' house can be difficult and costly, but for those who feel that a house can be attractively furnished in antique style, it is possible to buy

Research your subject

If you decide to take up collecting dolls' houses, invest the time to research your hobby. Try to study some of the fine old examples that are exhibited in museums and historic houses all over the world.

It is also a good idea to join a collectors' club through which you will meet fellow dolls' house enthusiasts who will undoubtedly be a valuable source of advice and information. You may also be able to swap furnishing odds and ends.

Read books and magazines on dolls' houses. It is well worth subscribing to the magazine *International dolls' House News*, which is full of the latest information about dolls' houses and miniature fairs, meetings of collectors, and suppliers of everything from knitting and sewing patterns for making your own dolls to bed linen for the miniature bedroom.

Old catalogues can also be a fascinating and useful source of reference. For example, in 1793, the German toy seller Georg Bestelmeier issued nine instalments of his catalogue of toys, each of which was fully described and illustrated with beautifully drawn copperplate engravings. These catalogues provide a rich mine of information about what was available during the late eighteenth and early nineteenth century, not only in Germany but in the rest of Europe to which the toys were exported.

Where to find dolls' houses

Dolls' houses can be found at antique fairs and in antique shops, auction rooms at specialist toy sales and even at car-boot sales.

RIGHT The sheer range of items that can be used to fill a dolls' house make collecting and furnishing dolls' houses an engrossing hobby.

CHAPTER ONE

SHOPS AND ROOMS

• • • •

S hops are a fairly recent development in our civilization. Until the eighteenth century merchants often traded from their homes and this was reflected in the dolls' houses of the period. In the lower parts of the Stromer house, dated 1639, and the Baumler house in Germany, for example, there are shelves and drawers packed with goods for scales and scales for weighing them out.

Notable examples

Model shops were produced and filled with stock of all kinds, some of it realistically modelled in wax. These delightful reminders of a long-vanished everyday life can be seen in many toy museums throughout Europe. Occasionally they appear on the market.

In the National museum in Germany there is what is probably the oldest separate shop of about the mid-eighteenth century which, compared with the elegant shops of later years, is a fairly rough model. It is a small wooden box with paper stars pasted on it and on two-storeys, with a male shopkeeper above and a female

shopkeeper below. The toy goods offered for sale are blocks of wood, painted in primary colours.

In 1696, the Dauphin of France had 'nine shops of the market place, filled with little pieces of enamel', which may have been market stalls. This simple form of shop turns up again and again in museums all over the world. The market woman from the Simon van Gijn museum in Dordrecht, the Netherlands, is an interesting early example of this kind of shop. Dated about 1820, the

ABOVE The conveniently small size of miniature shops and rooms may be one of the reasons why they were made in Europe in the nineteenth century.

ABOVE A miniature wooden shop from the Stadtmuseum, Munich. All the goods on display are modelled in wax.

wooden-headed doll stands behind her stall selling a variety of domestic utensils such as mops, shovels, brooms, and salt and knife boxes.

The Bethnal Green Museum of Childhood has an early market stall dated 1830, which they call a dolls' bazaar. The woman figure is selling haberdashery, including ribbons, reticules, pictures, packets of pins and a large doll. She is a close relative of the well known pedlar dolls so popular in Victorian days and seen in countless collections. Often the name of the pedlar and the date was written in ink on a piece of paper and pinned to the tray, just as the real-life pedlars of the time had to display their names on their licence-to-sell.

German production

Germans shops produced during the nineteenth century are delightfully imaginative and varied. There are millinery shops, with small dolls' heads showing off the bonnets and hats for sale; drapers' stores with cloth and drawers overflowing with buttons, ribbons and reels of thread; pottery shops with rows and rows of tiny jugs and bowls; flower shops; and dozens of others which are equally charming. The shapes of the miniature shops are as varied as the goods being sold; some look just like real shops with counters and shelves; others are in boxes with flaps that open out to reveal the goods inside.

Miniature market places with stalls were a speciality of southern Germany, and they were sold in boxed sets which could be built up by children, who could move from stall to stall buying what they wished. Others, such as the twentieth century copy of an earlier design from Erzgebirge in the toy museum at Sonneberg, had their goods stuck to the stalls, which made them less satisfactory as toys.

Some excellent examples of toy shops can be seen in the Toy Museum in Nuremberg. One is a millinery shop of about 1820, selling bonnets displayed on little papier mâché models, along with reticules, chemisettes, handkerchiefs, pictures with hooks to hold keys, and a mask to be worn at a ball. A sweet shop offers 'humbugs from Sweet Tooth and Co', 'London Peppermints' and jars full of jams and jellies. A basket shop dating from 1858 displays the wide range of handmade baskets that were available at the time and the variety of designs with which they were decorated. Some of the goods on show are hand-painted.

Grocery shops were also educational toys, teaching children how to trade, how to use money and give the right change. They could be very spectacular, one offering jars, packages, bottles and tins of labelled biscuits, sauces, tea, coffee, cheese, bread, fish and sweets, backed up by a formidable array of drawers containing dry goods labelled 'Anis', 'Nelken', 'Ilvanille', 'Niisse', 'Zimt', 'Nudeln', and so on. All these items were free-standing, so that a child could have a wonderful time taking them out and playing with them.

Fashion and millinery shops were particularly popular during the latter part of the nineteenth century, and they contained caps, veils, shawls, gowns with accessories, jabots, collars, cuffs, belts and stays, not to mention embroidered bell pulls, cushion covers, braces and suspenders, starched collars and shirt fronts for men. Everything had its rightful place on a shelf, a hanger or in a drawer.

BELOW A market scene made in Germany in the 1920s in the Sonneberg area.

RIGHT In the 19th century in England butcher's shops were a popular theme for miniature makers.

One giant shop, Zind's drapery store, dated 1875–80, in the Munich Stacitmuseum is a three-storey building which opens to reveal six rooms crammed with goods, neatly stacked and guarded by assistants standing behind long counters. The windows display goods. It is so detailed that it may have been a display piece for a shop window.

French shops

French shops were no less elaborate in the latter part of the nineteenth century. Many French shops are to be seen in the catalogues of Au Bon marché, where we see a later version of the fairground wheel, a fortune stall, and a grande épicerie, well stocked with packets, barrels and sacks of goods.

Modern French toy shops have been changed to keep up with the times. A 1987 catalogue from the Centre de Documentation du Jouet shows a sort of supermarket counter with cash register, scales, telephone, basket, change, and fruit and vegetables. Another toy is a cafeteria with cups and saucers, and as a final touch of realism, a vending machine dispensing chocolate!

English shops

Typical nineteenth century English shops tended to be butcher's shops. There are variations of butcher's shops in different museums; some are made with living quarters above, others are made like little boxes presided over by a figure in a striped apron standing beneath festoons of meat. An American 1899 Christmas catalogue of the John Wanamaker stores depicts a poultry shop with living quarters above. Several butcher's shops are shown in the Gamages catalogues from the early twentieth century.

More modern shops

The tradition of dolls' shops has continued into the twentieth century. A fine-quality milliner's shop in the Bethnal Green Museum of Childhood was produced in the 1920s. Many children growing up in the 1930s can recall the magic of their first sweet shop with its little glass jars of dolly mixtures and the grocer's shop.

Cecil Coleman Ltd of London advertised a Peter Pan Store for sixpence in 1933. It was a large folding shop. Printed in attractive colours and came complete with miniatures filled with sweets, scale, scoop, invoices and bags.

The firm of Tri-ang produced two shops in 1951: one with bright modern decor, complete with revolving door, counters and display shelves; another with an apartment above for the owner – all very modern.

That craft workers of today are well aware of the attraction of miniature shops is shown in the lovely toy shop made by the late Yootha Rose, and the antique shop by Joan Gibson, made in the 1980s.

The modern craftsman Frank Egerton also produces butchers' shops in which all the joints of meat can be detached from their hooks.

Dutch shops

A variation on the usual run of shops is seen in Holland, where in the Simon van Gijn museum there is an attractive Tabak, Snuif, Koffij, Thee shop in which these goods are displayed in large drums, as presumably they were in real life in the nineteenth century.

BELOW This English cardboard shop probably dates from about 1890.

THE CARLISLE COLLECTION

The Carlisle Collection of miniature rooms was the lifetime hobby of the late Mrs F. M. Carlisle, the wife of a wealthy businessman and a mother of four children, who began her hobby of collecting antique miniatures in 1921.

By 1933, Mrs Carlisle's collection had become well established, and she commissioned crafts-men to make rooms for some of her pieces. There is a Regency games room, for example, which was made for her growing collection of miniature games, and an Adam music room for a set of Japanese instruments.

Later, she had craftsmen make fine furniture to go in the rooms, giving them a more realistic appearance, and this is how the collection came to be formed. She herself made petit point carpets and upholstery to fit in with the period of each of the rooms.

Modern collectors are still having rooms made for their treasures, or making them themselves. The museum at Stony Brook, Long Island, U.S.A., has 15 rooms designed, made and furnished by Frederick Hicks, who was inspired by the Thorne rooms, and the Gibbes Art Gallery in Charleston, South Carolina, has a permanent exhibition of ten miniature period rooms by Elizabeth Wallace, eight of them miniature replicas of rooms in historic American homes.

In England, a fine model of the drawing room at Sledmere House, near Driffield, Humberside, was made by Royston Jones and Fiona Gray in 1985 and featured in the magazine *International dolls' House News* in the autumn issue of 1988.

ABOVE LEFT Mrs Carlisle, the creator of the collection of miniature rooms at Nunnington Hall, Yorkshire, England.

BELOW This finely detailed Palladian entrance hall was the last of the Carlisle rooms to be made.

Shops made of paper

Paper shops were being made in Germany in the mid-nineteenth century. In her book *Collecting dolls' houses and Miniatures*, Norah Earnshaw shows a folding paper dress shop, containing four paper dolls and a table with four bonnets on it. When not in use, the room folded into its box. By the end of the nineteenth century, brightly colored folding cardboard shops were sold with cut-out paper customers.

Miniature rooms

Miniature rooms were made in France and Germany as long ago as the seventeenth century. In 1607 Heroard, physician to the young Dauphin of France, recorded dolls' rooms from the early years of the seventeenth century, which belonged to the Dauphin's sisters.

The writer D'Allemagne describes how in 1675 a gilded room containing a four-poster bed was given to the Duc de Maine by Madame Thianges inscribed "Ta Chambre du Sublime".

Cardinal Richelieu presented the Princess d'Enghien with a model intended as a toy, which showed a mother lying in a bed surrounded by a nursemaid, midwife and grandmother. Reputedly, the young Princess was told that she was allowed dress and undress the dolls in this room, but that she could not bath the baby, because it was made of wax.

Learning through play

Shops and rooms were often used to teaching housewifely tasks. Miniature kitchens, were a popular gift to a girl as long ago as 1572, when the Princess of Saxony was given one. Toy kitchens were especially popular in Germany, where even middle-class girls were expected to be familiar with the work of the kitchen. Models kitchens in the Nuremberg tradition such as the one in the Metropolitan Museum of Art, New York were made well into the twentieth century. They give a fascinating insight into life of the period. Originally they were wood, with copper and pewter utensils, but gradually they became smaller in size and were made of tin.

Several toy kitchens can be seen in the toy museum, Nuremberg. One is a well equipped Franconian kitchen, dating from 1830 – with a metal utensils, a flat iron with a heating block inside, a drum for roasting coffee, an earthenware roasting pot and a stand for beer-mugs.

BELOW William Randolph Hearst, the American newspaper magnate owned this detailed kitchen, which includes irons, breadboards, a poacher, a roaster and a teakettle among its array of kitchen paraphernalia.

The style of kitchens changed as the years went by. A kitchen made in 1905 by Marklin has one of the first electric stoves. It came complete with a cookery book, a hay box for keeping food hot and the light blue enamel vessels which were popular about that time.

There are some fine examples of rooms in various German museums. In the toy museum at Nuremberg, the earliest is a seventeenth century set of three rooms, including a kitchen, living room and bedroom.

RIGHT The roof and front of this French school room open to reveal the class and schoolmistress within. Reports and notebooks adorn the roof and walls.

Another set of two dolls' rooms is later in date, with a large drawing room and a narrow bedchamber, in the Biedermeier style, which had originated in Austria and Germany during the years 1814–48. This word was coined from the German words Bieder, meaning plain or unpretentious, and Meier, a common German surname. Its graceful uncluttered lines are a pleasant change from earlier, heavier styles of furniture.

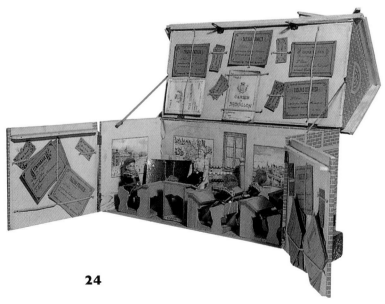

French rooms

There are several dolls' rooms in the Musée du Jouet at Poissy, near Paris. One shows a bride and groom in a bedroom with furniture made of pine twigs. Another is an elegantly furnished salon, with silken curtains and upholstered chairs. Other typically French rooms were laundries and stables. Schoolrooms too were a particularly French interest and were produced well into the twentieth century.

The Thorne Rooms

The sixty-eight famous Thorne rooms were created by Mrs James Ward Thorne of Indiana, USA, who began collecting miniatures as a young girl at the end of the nineteenth century. Later, motivated by a mission to educate the public in architecture, interior design and the visual arts, Mrs Ward set out to create a set of miniature rooms which would illustrate a comprehensive history of European and American interior design. Skilled craftsmen made the rooms according to her plans and she provided many of the miniatures from her own collection.

The rooms are interiors dating from 1500 to 1940, with the majority representing the eighteenth century. Many are copies of rooms in historic houses or museums, while others combine features copied from houses and palaces seen by Mrs Thorne during her travels abroad. There are 31 European rooms and 37 American rooms, In 1941 Mrs Thorne presented them all to the Art Institute of Chicago, where they are on public display.

CHAPTER TWO

NOTABLE SEVENTEENTH AND EIGHTEENTH CENTURY HOUSES

● ● ● ●

The earliest dolls' house (or baby house as it would have been called then) still in existence is dated 1611. This heavy, wooden cabinet built in the shape of a house, 2.75 m (9 ft) high, 1.8m (6ft) wide and 0.6m (2ft) deep is in the Germanisches National Museum, Germany. The base of the house is the cellar, and the ground floor contains a Great Hall and a yard with a triple gallery, and a garden.

Stairs from the yard lead to the second floor, where there is a delightful kitchen containing a vast array of utensils and a living room, which was modernized in the eighteenth century. A bedroom on the top floor contains a huge bed, and a stateroom.

The Stromer house

The 1639 house known as the Stromer house, can be seen in the Germanisches National Museum. The house was named after the last owner, Baron von Stromer. At a little under 2.1m (7ft) high, it is slightly smaller than the 1611 house, and it contains over a thousand objects which provide a unique picture of domestic life in a prosperous seventeenth century German household.

RIGHT Dated 1611, this is the earliest known dolls' house still in existence. It has two halls, five rooms and a cellar and garden. This 2.75m (9ft) tall dolls' house can be seen at the Germanisches Nationalmuseum, Germany.

*RIGHT Two adults
and a baby
occupy a bedroom,
furnished with a
four poster bed
and a cradle in
the Baumler house
in the
Germanisches
National Museum.*

In this building the two sets of four workrooms on either side of the main entrance demonstrate how self-contained such large dwellings were, housing a byre complete with animals, a wine store, general store and a shop with an office, and a laundry as well as servants' rooms and a nursery.

The kitchen on the first floor is lavishly equipped. The focal point of the kitchen was the fire. The fireplace is deep, with a chimney large enough to smoke meat, and there is a spit and a clockwork jack for roasting meat. There are also weights and a noticeboard.

There are also two comfortable bedrooms with large curtained, cushioned beds and ceramic stoves, and a reception room.

*BELOW The
Baumler house
has a merchant's
room on the
bottom floor.
Goods, such as
paper and cheese
are arranged on
the shelves.*

The Kress House

The Kress house, in the same museum, dates from the latter part of the seventeenth century. It is populated by a family and staff of eighteenth century dolls. There are stables and storerooms, and four family rooms, a kitchen, reception room and two bedrooms.

The Baumlerhoues

The Baumler house, dating from the later part of the seventeenth century, is also inhabited by family and servants, and it has an interesting central hallway with a painted vista. The drawing room is particularly elegant, full of little ornaments, paintings and finely dressed dolls. In fact, all the detail of this house is carefully observed, from the brass cooking pots in the kitchen, to the baby's cradle, the birdcage and the carved ivory bracket.

Ann Sharp's House

During the same period in England, between the year 1691 and the first part of the eighteenth century, a much less elaborate baby house was made for Ann

KING'S LYNN BABY HOUSE

The King's Lynn baby house (made in about 1740) was found with only its original panelling, door and fireplaces, but perhaps what it lacks in furniture is made up for by its interesting history. It is a replica in miniature of 27 King Street, King's Lynn, Norfolk, England once the home of a Dutch merchant named Flierden and his wife, who had the baby house built for their child, Ann.

In the 1920s a local dignitary gave the baby house to a Torquay children's home run by the Children's Society. Before that it had been kept somewhere in Bath. The house was restored in 1984 by Vivien Greene and a group of craftswomen who furnished the two bedrooms, dining room, music room, kitchen and counting house with modern furniture in a style suitable to the period and in accord with the Flierdens' Quaker beliefs. More recently the house has been on display at Powderham Castle, near Exeter, in Devon.

ABOVE. The counting house in the King's Lynn baby house was furnished simply because the merchant was a Quaker.

LEFT. The King's Lynn baby house was modelled on number 27 King Street, King's Lynn England.

RIGHT. The King's Lynn baby house had only its original panelling, door and fireplaces when it was rescued.

Sharp, daughter of the Archbishop of York, and god-daughter of Queen Anne. This house was intended as a plaything, not as an educational aid or an adult's amusement. It is a quite roughly constructed cabinet.

The house has been preserved more or less as Ann left it and it contains some very interesting miniatures and curios, and a household of dolls, each with its name on a slip of paper pinned to its clothing. The cast includes 'Sarah Gill, ye child's maid', and 'Roger, ye butler', as well as 'Lady Jemima Johnson' and 'Lord Rochett'.

In the nursery a walnut cradle contains a wax baby, a large baby basket, a four-legged stool holding a silver saucepan for warming the baby's food, a pair of ivory

candlesticks and a paper dolls' house, perhaps made by Ann Sharp. The boudoir, contains a wax-relief portrait of Mother Shipton, a witch born in 1486, and a delicately carved chandelier in a glass sphere and a pet monkey wearing a flat hat, sitting on a chair.

In the centre of the cabinet is the hall, which also serves as the dining room and next to the hall is the kitchen containing the fireplace with a pig roasting on a spit, bellows, a plate warmer and cooking utensils. The reception room, on the other side of the hall, is occupied by Lady Jemima, Mrs Lemon and Lord Rochett. 'Mrs Hannah, ye housekeeper' occupies a moderately well furnished room beneath the reception room. The other two basement rooms are a servants' hall and a storeroom.

BELOW In the Ann Sharp house the hallway doubles as the dining room. The lady of the house is on her way downstairs and the butler is standing by the door.

Dutch Baby Cabinets

Towards the end of the seventeenth century and into the eighteenth century the Dutch developed a great enthusiasm for collecting baby cabinets. These cabinets were not intended as playthings, but were the hobby of wealthy merchants' wives, who have left these enchanting legacies for us to enjoy in Dutch museums.

Petronella de la Court

Housed in the Centraal Museum in Utrecht, this is a late seventeenth century dolls' house which is quite different in feel from the German cabinets, reflecting as it does the sophisticated yet comfortable lifestyle of the prosperous Dutch merchants. The little rooms are furnished in luxury, filled with artistic treasures just as their real-life rooms would have been, the figures enjoying this civilized ambience clothed in rich silks and laces.

The Sara Ploos van Amstel cabinet

Dutch cabinets reached their peak in the eighteenth century, with the lovely Sara Ploos van Amstel cabinet in the Gemeente museum, The Hague. It is on three levels, and the rooms are in boxes surrounded by borders or frames. Mrs van Amstel left copious notes and kept all her invoices while furnishing her cabinet, so we know that she bought three old dolls' cabinets at auction in 1743 and transferred rooms from these to the new cabinet. Some of the boxes had belonged to the artist David van der Plaats, who painted murals on the music-room walls, some of the canvas carpets and the ceilings.

Two small rooms under the eaves are a curio room and a bedroom. On the middle floor there is a magnificent porcelain room. The music room on this floor has painted walls and contains silver miniatures of all kinds, and a full complement of musical instruments and games. In the basement is a richly furnished lying-in room (a feature of most Dutch dolls' houses in an age when married women spent much of their time producing children) and a kitchen.

The Blaaw House

The exterior of the Blaaw house, which was also once owned by Sara Ploos van Amstel and is kept in the Frans Hals Museum, in Haarlem, takes us away from the

ABOVE A walnut cradle holds a baby in the Ann Sharp house's nursery. The paper dolls' house is an unusual item.

29

THE UPPARK BABY HOUSE

A huge eighteenth century masterpiece is housed at Uppark, in England. Uppark itself was partially destroyed by fire in 1989, but the elegant dolls' house which was brought to her new home by Sarah Lethieullier when she went there as the bride of Sir Matthew Fetherstonhaugh in 1747, was fortunately saved for posterity.

The baby house has been left untouched, so its beautiful Queen Anne exterior and its nine rooms on three floors, each room opening separately, are a perfect time-capsule of life in a great country house some 250 years ago. There are delicate architectural details such as brass doorlocks and knobs, panelled walls and marble fireplaces with brass firegrates. The furnishings are simple and graceful and probably date a little earlier than the baby house.

The inhabitants of the house conform to the early-eighteenth century convention that servants were made with wooden heads while the gentry were made of wax and dressed in fine clothes. Each lady wears the correct cap and gown, and even the right number of petticoats; the gentleman of the house wears fashionable clothes and a powdered wig, and he carries a sword at his side, as was the custom for men at this time. The family is seated in the parlour taking tea and the dining room table, attended by liveried footmen, is laid for a meal with silver table settings under a silver chandelier.

As in the Dutch baby houses, there is a lying-in room, occupied by a mother and nurse, and dotted about the house are miniature paintings, some of which may have been painted by Lady Sarah herself, for she was an accomplished artist.

LEFT A portrait of Sarah Lethieullier who brought her baby house to Uppark, England during the 18th century.

BELOW The Uppark house is a beautifully furnished, large structure containing nine rooms on three floors.

A fashion catches on in England

Eighteenth century Europe soon took up the craze for baby houses. In England, even royalty is said to have dabbled in the new craze. Frederick, Prince of Wales, took up the hobby after visiting the miniature town of Mon Plaisir. English baby houses usually looked like real houses. Some had handles for travelling, but others were too large to move.

Nostell Priory baby house

Kept in West Yorkshire, England this is a perfect example of the grand style of English dolls' house. It was commissioned in 1735 by Sir Rowland Winn and designed

LEFT Opaque glass is painted to look like china in the porcelain room of the Sara Ploos van Amstel cabinet house.

BELOW In the silver room in the Sara Blaaw house a recess at the rear displays the family's silverware.

cabinet to the representation of a real house. The interior decoration reaches new heights of craftsmanship. The house contains twelve rooms on four floors, counting the halls, and is filled with exquisite silver, basketware, miniature paintings, tables, chairs, glassware, and pottery. It holds a family and staff of wax dolls.

On the next floor the silver room is full of sparkling silver for which Dutch silversmiths were renowned. The study of Dr Ludeman, astrologer and physician, contains items of his professions such as medicine bottles and books. The other rooms are a music room, a lying-in room, laundry rooms and a man's bedroom.

Other examples

Not all Dutch baby houses were for the rich. A charming little eighteenth century cabinet house can be seen at the Simon van Gijn museum in Dordrecht. It has only five rooms including a typically Dutch kitchen.

by his architect James Paine, who based it on the real Nostell Priory. The rooms have carved panelling and mouldings, each fender is separately designed. The period furniture is said to have been made by the famous furniture maker Thomas Chippendale, and the rooms were decorated by Lady Winn and her sister. The small parlour is decorated with Chinese wallpaper.

The Tare baby house

The Tare baby house, dated 1760 (named after its donor, Mrs Walter Tare), is in the Bethnal Green Museum of Childhood. The exterior has an accurate facade and double staircase leading to a pedimented front door. Four rooms are visible through the windows – a bedroom, dining room and two reception rooms.

There is also a kitchen in the basement which can only be seen when the sections of the house are separated. The house was modernized and updated in 1830.

The house at Strangers' Hall

Strangers' Hall in Norwich has a solid wooden house with carrying handles, dated about 1720. The outside of the house is painted to look like brickwork, and it is clearly a toy that has been played with by children.

The Yarburgh baby house

The Castle Museum in York has the Yarburgh baby house, dated about 1751 and made for the children of the Heslington family. It consists of nine rooms, each opening independently.

RIGHT The well-equipped kitchen in the 18th century dolls' house at Stranger's Hall, England. The hastener on the left of the fireplace was used for cooking meat.

CHAPTER THREE

NINETEENTH CENTURY
DOLLS' HOUSES

● ● ● ●

Some of the characteristics of the previous century linger on in the early nineteenth century houses; kitchens have huge fireplaces with spit racks and big built-in dressers, the latter remaining a feature right up to the end of the nineteenth century.

The nineteenth century saw an enormous degree of social change. Britain became strong and confident in possession of a powerful empire, and life on the American continent was well established. The middle classes expanded. They no longer worked at home but went to offices, factories and other business premises. Their increased earning power enabled them to turn their homes into treasure houses to display a range of taste and wealth. To satisfy this desire for possessions, mass production made goods in all manner of historical, styles (then known as revival, styles). The emphasis was on possessions and home comfort. and family life was all-important.

With the new significance of their homes, the middle classes gave enormous attention to furnishing and decoration. Magazines and books on household decorative design and etiquette were available for guidance as so many aspects were involved in creating the desired impression. The home became a monument to family and achievement and this is reflected in the dolls' houses of the period.

BELOW The kitchen became the middle-class housewife's pride and joy.

ABOVE The kitchen of a dolls' house made by the Nuremberg toy maker Christian Hacker c1900.

Germany

Germany in the nineteenth century was noted more for the quality and variety of the dolls'-house furniture, produced there and exported around the world, than for the dolls' houses themselves. However there were some manufacturers of note.

Christian Hacker and Co

A famous German manufacturer named Christian Hacker, who was working towards the end of the nineteenth century and early twentieth, specialized in attractive French-looking houses with mansard roofs, some with a central staircase. It was a style of dolls' house which was to remain popular until the 1930s.

Christian Hacker and Co was a firm of toymakers founded in Nuremburg in 1870. Their trademark, registered in 1875, was a distinctive one of the intertwined initials 'CH' with a little crown on top.

This firm had a great influence on the design of later nineteenth century Continental houses. Indeed variations on the Christian Hacker style appeared for many years. A characteristic feature of the style is the line decoration on the cream-painted furniture. It is particularly noticeable in the kitchens, where it is often applied to dressers and fireplaces.

Some of the Christian Hacker houses open out on one side to reveal four rooms, hall and staircase, others open in two sections with a roof that lifts off and instead

The Victorian era

Perhaps the most popular concept of an ideal dolls' house is an elaborate Victorian plaything. The Victorian period lasted over 60 years Queen Victoria reigned in England from 1837 until 1901. Popular taste altered frequently and the era combined some new concepts with traditional designs, reshaping them into novel forms which became known as 'Victorian'.

HALLWAYS

The necessary furniture required would be racks for hats, coats, canes and umbrellas. Other pieces might be straight-backed chairs, sofas, benches, hall tables and perhaps a carved chest. Accessories might include: flower vases, plants, a grandfather clock, a barometer, a boot scraper, a visiting card tray, a telephone and family pictures or small etchings on the wall.

BELOW A view into the drawing room across the hallway.

RIGHT A ceramic gold coloured pot holds a painted paper plant.

ABOVE Sun slants across the wooden hallway floor, and a grandfather clock ticks away the hours.

BELOW A handworked miniature rug with a flower motif.

The hall was given as much decorative attention as the other rooms in the house. It was the first part of the house that a visitor would see. Americans favoured a more informal style of decoration than the English.

of a staircase there is an extra room. In addition the facades of the houses vary too; some of them have balconies, others pillars.

BELOW A fine dolls' house c1880 from the Musée des Arts Décoratifs, Paris, with a typical mansard roof.

A contemporary girls' magazine tells us that Christian Hacker did market research in England when he was exploring the English market, and he copied houses in London, but the most well known style is French.

The French style

There is a house in the Musée des Arts et Traditions Populaires in Paris, which is furnished in typically French style, full of elegant silk hangings and white and gold furniture. The exterior is very like the Christian Hacker house, with its mansard roof and central balcony but it stands in its own balustraded garden and the front is decorated with orange lozenges.

Another typically French style of house, known as the Deauville house, began to appear towards the end of the nineteenth century. Deauville houses are small, rather like seaside boarding houses, with bay windows and steps up to the front door. They usually stand on a base which is painted to look like rock. The villas have two rooms and lithographed bricks and wallpaper.

Denmark

Copenhagen boasts several dolls' houses which can be seen in Legoland and in the Dansk Folkemuseum, which has more than twenty. Among these is the Villa Olga, a tall, narrow building in Danish Renaissance style, with ten windows in the front. There are four floors, the top and bottom floors opening separately, the middle two floors opening together. The bottom floor contains two storerooms, on the ground floor is a kitchen, on the third a salon, and on the top is a bedroom. The maids' rooms would have been in the attics.

DINING ROOM

The dining room would be situated on the ground floor adjacent to the kitchen. It was an important room in which to impress guests and walls were often covered in slightly masculine, dark papers or deep wood panelling. This was a room that was used almost exclusively in the evening, and it would be lit with lamps and warmed by a fire in an imposing fireplace.

A dining table and chairs (between six and twelve) would dominate the room, and there was usually a sideboard, on which a range of dishes and ornaments would be displayed. The wall coverings would

ABOVE A glass decanter and wine glasses may have sat on a side table.

RIGHT A sombre, quite masculine English dining room.

be protected by a chair rail around the room. Chair seats were often leather, which was less likely to retain the odour of food than fabric.

Further items of dining room furniture may be a sofa, a plant stand, a secondary sideboard, and a range of smaller side tables, usually in dark wood.

LEFT A dining room window with a trompe l'oeil pelmet design. Tea things are set out to one side.

RIGHT A side table is used to display Christmas items in a 19th century dining room.

ABOVE This
Swedish dolls'
house is dated
around 1856.
It was arranged
by Mrs Emily
Kihlberg for her
13 children.

house containing six rooms furnished in Swedish Victorian style, with a family of dolls all warmly wrapped up against the cold. Some of the furniture is German.

Finland

The Museovirasto in Helsinki, Finland, has several dolls' houses, the earliest of which, dated 1830, is a mixture of styles and sizes, and the Aina Friedman house, which was made for a merchant's daughter of that name in about 1860. The furniture was either home-made or imported from Germany, as the manufacture of dolls'-house furniture did not begin in Finland until late in the nineteenth century.

Switzerland

Switzerland has several nineteenth century houses, in the Historisches Museum, Basel. The most famous is the five-storey house made in 1850 by the Basel artist Ludwig Adam Kelterborn for his three daughters. This detailed cabinet house can be viewed from both sides. It has an attic, a laundry and a storage room on the ground floor, six other rooms and cellars, as well as a large central staircase with doors leading onto two balcony rooms. The windows at the sides of the building ensure that this house is well lit and the effect is one of well ordered, Swiss domesticity.

Sweden

Dolls' houses were also popular in Scandinavian countries in the nineteenth century. Some were locally made, while others were imported from Germany. The Nordiska Museet in Stockholm has the Emily Kihlberg

DRAWING ROOM

Tables of various sizes and styles were used in the drawing room throughout the period. They were often quite elaborate and expensive and were usually decorated with vases of flowers or other ornaments. An ornate fireplace would dominate the room, and a large mirror often hung above it. The walls would be hung with the householder's best pictures.

LEFT The drawing room was the place where musical entertainment would take place in the evening, often with the whole family joining in.

RIGHT An ornate, marble topped 'D' table adorned with a collection of Russian lacquer boxes.

The drawing room was traditionally the room to which the ladies withdrew after dinner, leaving the men at the dining table. It would be furnished in a feminine style. The drawing room was usually the largest in the house with a large window. it was the main entertaining and and reception room and the furniture would be comfortable and costly. It would often be crammed with furniture, partly to offer plenty of seating and partly as a form of display.

LEFT Oriental artefacts such as this cloisonné vase were very fashionable items of drawing room furniture.

RIGHT This exquisite Victorian parlour can be seen at the Toy and Miniature Museum of Kansas City.

RIGHT The
Cockthorpe Hall
dolls' house was
owned by one
child then passed
onto her daughter
who is now in
her eighties.

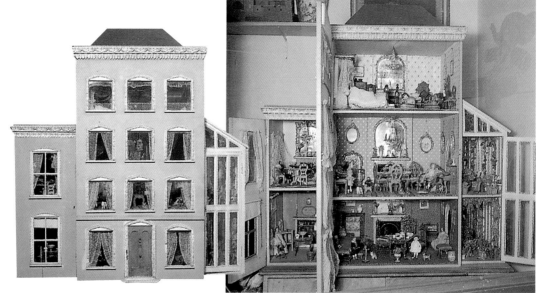

England

Nineteenth century English dolls' houses give us a good, if idealized, picture of the life of the country's more prosperous citizens. Here are the toy-filled nurseries, busy kitchens, well-laid tables, over crowded drawing rooms and stuffy bedrooms which were familiar to most of the middle and upper classes. In the nineteenth century dolls' houses were once again fashionable, not as collectors' showpieces, but as children's toys.

Children's toys

It was easy to furnish dolls' houses at this time because toy shops were full of delightful imported German pieces to tempt children to part with their weekly pocket money. Many of the Victorian dolls' houses on view in museums are still furnished with ivory, bone and wood carvings from Berchtesgarten, tin furniture from Nuremburg and Wurttemburg, metal filigrée furniture from Diessen, glassware and pottery from Thuringia, and 'rosewood' furniture from Waltershausen.

Waltershausen furniture features frequently in nineteenth century English dolls' houses. It is strongly made, wooden and easily recognizable for its imitation ebony and gold, or rosewood and gold appearance. It comes in every possible shape and form, from marble-topped washstands to pianos and writing desks.

The Egerton Killer house

A dolls' house of dated 1835–8, can be seen in the Bethnal Green Museum of Childhood. It is housed in an 1800 lacquered cabinet but furnished in the style of the 1830s. The dolls and furnishings were gathered together, and some of them were made by the wife and daughters of John Egerton Killer, a Manchester man who, in defiance of his name, was a physician. It is a particularly beautifully made cabinet.

CONSERVATORY

The conservatory reached the height of its popularity at the end of the nineteenth century. It often led off a study or library. It would usually have a tiled floor and stained glass, panelled walls. Furniture was usually bamboo or wicker, with cast iron urns or wrought-iron garden seats.

Potted palms, tropical plants and exotic birds in cages created an atmosphere of relaxation. The conservatory provided the perfect place for the nineteenth century householder to indulge in the fashionable pastime of cultivating plants and flowers.

LEFT A miniature resin replica of a cast iron garden bench.

RIGHT An elaborate miniature glass house made with real glass. Conservatories were more usually attached to the house.

LEFT The conservatory was a relaxing place to take tea among exotic palms and plants in pots.

The Audley End house

A delightful English dolls' house which contains Waltershausen and other German and home-made furniture can be seen at Audley End in England. The dolls' house is quite roughly constructed, and is really no more than a series of boxes of assorted shapes and sizes, but it is crammed with all kinds of furniture and tiny objects and the children who furnished it clearly had a wonderful time doing so.

The fine gilt overmantels, pier glasses and elegant firegrates must have been professionally made, as were the pressed tin chairs and clock of a type known to collectors as 'Orly'. This orange-coloured furniture was thought until recently to have been made in Germany, but an article in *International dolls' House News* by Margaret Towner has established that the firm of Evans

and Cartwright of Wolverhampton, England (who were general toy manufacturers, factors and tinplate workers) probably made tin dolls' house furniture up until at least 1849, and the Orly products could well have come from this manufacturer.

Wooden pieces of furniture in the Audley End house include mahogany chests of drawers, dumb waiters (which carried food upstairs from the kitchen), a beautifully detailed upright piano with pleated silk panel, a delicate harp and a round table with simulated antler legs. This piece reflects the nineteenth century English fashion for horn furniture.

The home-made items, and the curtains, upholstered seats, embroidered footstools and needlepoint carpets are all a testimony to the diligence of the children.

BELOW RIGHT The Audley End house was brightly decorated, with wallpaper in most rooms. The paper was probably intended for lining drawers and chests.

BELOW The music room of the Audley End house has long red silk curtains. The delicate harp strings are still in place.

BEDROOM

The bedroom was a private room and the look would be individual and personal. Light colours were often favoured. After 1840 matching furniture suites became fashionable, comprising the bed, armoire, dressing bureau, commode and washstand. Beds were often highly decorated. There might also be a writing des,k, chairs, footstools, an ottoman, shelves, a mirror and a chaise longue.

RIGHT The master bedroom would usually hold one or two comfortably padded, decorative chairs.

BELOW A bed in the Victorian Renaissance revival style. The sheets and pillows are real English linen trimmed with lace. The green coverlet is pure silk.

RIGHT Before indoor plumbing every bedroom would have a washstand which held a pitcher and bowl. This corner stand also has a matching chamber pot.

BELOW A view of the bay window of a Victorian bedroom in a miniature Italianate villa in San Francisco from about 1882.

RIGHT The drawing room of Whiteway in the Rotunda collection, Oxford, England. The walls are covered in pale blue satin.

Whiteway house

Whiteway house, dated 1845, is in the Rotunda collection. This house was formerly at Saltram House, England. The owner, Lord Morley (who died in 1962), gave it to his footman for his small daughter.

When the National Trust took over Saltram House, the dolls' house had been sold to a local antique dealer; However, it has now been willed back to the National Trust, and can be seen by visitors to Saltram.

The original wallcoverings survive except in the hall and the linen room; the left-hand bedroom has some original furnishings including the bed with chintz hangings, the matching curtains and the handmade carpet decorated with rosebuds.

The drawing-room walls are covered in pale blue satin held in place by narrow gilt-metal fillets. The pictures have been added more recently together with a bead chair, a harp and a 'marble' table. Some of the toys in the schoolroom are recent, but most are mid-nineteenth century. The maps are neatly mounted and contemporary with the house, the music albums are copies of Victorian songs and there is a case containing ten hand-cut paper butterflies which tremble on tiny paper supports in a case less than 3.8cm (1½in) long.

The library books are made of carved wood and each one is different. The globe is a rarity, and is dated 1851. The fine carpet was already in the room, as was the table, the bible, and most of the furnishings. There are three figures and a dog in the library.

BATHROOM

With the advent of indoor plumbing in the last quarter of the nineteenth century, washstands in the bedroom could be given taps and permanently fixed bowls with plug holes and piping for the waste water. Bathtubs were also given a permanent fixed site. Early bathrooms were often converted from dressing-rooms or small bedrooms and were usually quite large. Bedroom furniture, such as dressers, side tables and even sofas followed the washstand into the new room.

Early fixtures were boxed in cabinets to disguise their real function. By 1880 water closets were part of the bathroom furniture, but they were often in a separate cubicle.

LEFT Water closets were often located on their own at the rear of the house.

ABOVE An earlier style of bathtub set in a panelled wooden cabinet.

ABOVE The first water closets in Victorian bathrooms were boxed in wooden cabinets to disguise their real function.

BELOW A ceramic bidet bowl.

RIGHT A gas powered water heater with enamel and brass fitting, for use in a Victorian bathroom.

RIGHT A
bedroom in the
Hammond House,
Northumberland,
England. The metal
bed, picture
frames and
fireplace are
probably German.

The Hammond house

At Wallington Hall in Northumberland, England there is a remarkable collection of fifteen or so dolls' houses dating from 1845 to 1930. The largest house in the collection is the Hammond house, which is a simple structure of box-like rooms, each filled with a lavish variety of commercially made furniture. When the house was unpacked, it was found to contain over 1,000 pieces of furniture, 256 pictures, 10 clocks and 77 dolls.

ABOVE The family
are assembled for
dinner in the
dining room of the
Hammond House.

There are 36 rooms in all, inhabited by a family of china-headed dolls. The house was lit by electricity when it was built and water was piped from tanks on the roof to the bathroom and scullery below. All the wallpapers in the house are original and in some cases, they have been hand-painted.

Smaller nineteenth century dolls' houses

The houses mentioned so far are some of the larger Victorian houses, belonging to children of wealthy families, but by the end of the century there were also plenty of humble dolls' houses on the market.

Sometimes these little treasures appear in auction rooms. In 1988 Christies of South Kensington, London sold Gracie Cottage, a two-roomed dolls' house. In 1910 the matron of Greenwich Royal Infirmary asked the hall porter to make a doll's house using a wooden shoe box. The result was Gracie Cottage, a miniature house, with interior furniture, fixtures and fittings. The exterior of the house was painted with flowers.

Early Gamages catalogues show the huge variety of small dolls' houses being sold at about this time. Some of the cheaper houses were made of cardboard. The English Toy Company set up in 1889 made Miss Dollie Daisy Dimple's Villa, which could be taken to pieces and packed flat for transit or storage, and be rebuilt.

KITCHEN

The kitchen was essentially a place of work. Plain off-white walls and a scrubbed floor were the norm. This was the domain of the servants so ornamentation was usually at a minimum. There would be a scullery for household chores, and pantries for storing china, equipment and foods.

By the 1870s, particularly in America, more consideration was given to the people who worked in the kitchen. Ease of cleanliness, efficiency and a cheerfulness became more important factors. Rag rugs, carpet pieces or decorated oilcloths might be used to soften the appearance.

Wooden ice boxes became increasingly popular. There would be a large central table and a plumbed in sink. Essential items included: pastry board, rolling pin, grinding machine, scales, iron or copper pots, kettle, knives and choppers.

ABOVE The kitchen would be fitted out with a range of pots and pans, such as the cast iron set above, and other equipment to help the housewife.

LEFT A bright, clean looking American kitchen from after the Civil War. Decoration was kept to a minimum.

RIGHT A small labelled spice cabinet, designed to be hung on the wall.

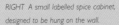

RIGHT Gracie
cottage was
handmade by the
hall porter of the
Greenwich
Infirmary, London,
England. It was
sold in 1989 at
auction for £1,540

Cottage workers, some of them children, made up these toys at home. 'The most competent of whom are able to earn as much as 17 shillings a week. The youngsters in their homes find very congenial employment in building up dolls' houses', says the advertisement, and the English Toy Company does them good service in enabling them to earn a few shillings weekly, at the same time keeping them out of mischief.

USA

In their 1875–6 catalogue, the firm of McLaughlin in the USA listed a folding dolls' house made of two pieces of printed straw board which slotted together to form a four-roomed apartment, each room 1.33m (4ft 3in) square. They produced several other imaginative designs. One had a set of lithographed paper furniture to go with it; and later there was a house with a fold-down cardboard garden. These cardboard houses give us a vivid picture of the popular style of interior decoration.

LEFT A typical Baltimore mansion from about 1870. It is an impressive multi-storey house with eight rooms.

There was no mass production of dolls' houses in the USA in the first part of the nineteenth century, so those that survive from this early period are handmade. The Brett house in the Museum of the City of New York, for example, gives a perfect picture of life in a comfortable American home in about 1838. The same museum has the refined Shelton Taylor house, with Biedermeier interiors.

Rupert Bliss

For each miniature masterpiece, there were hundreds of simple boxes made by American fathers for their children, or by manufacturers. The most famous of these was Rupert Bliss, who was established as a toymaker in 1832. The dolls' houses for which he was most famous were the lithograph-on-paper ones. Schoenhut and Converse also produced colour-printed dolls' houses but their style is not as distinctive as that of Bliss.

CHAPTER FOUR

DOLLS' HOUSES OF THE TWENTIETH CENTURY

● ● ● ●

This century has, on the whole, been the age of the smaller manufactured dolls' house, sold at a reasonable price. Individual craftsmen have also produced dolls' houses of a high standard.

American manufacturers

After the turn of the century, the toy-manufacturing industry in the USA became well established. Prominent among the toymakers was the firm of Rufus Bliss, who was born in 1802. He set up as a carpenter in 1825, founding his own business a few years later making wooden parts for pianos. The earliest advertisement listing Bliss toys appeared in 1871, and the firm carried on making toys, under other names, until 1935.

By 1907, the firm was making an extensive line of dolls' houses, all in a late-Victorian style. They were richly decorated and embellished with gables, porches, balconies and pillars. Some had isinglass windows and lace curtains; others had lithographed windows. The houses were compact. Some were made of heavy board hinged with cloth, so that they could be folded away.

The Bliss company produced lithographed paper-on-wood houses which had brightly coloured facades and 'tiled' roofs and porches. The distinctive style was then imitated in France and other European countries as well as by other American manufacturers such as Schoenhut and Converse.

BELOW Two 20th century dolls houses made of lithographed paper on wood.

BELOW The US
firm of Rufus Bliss
made this small
dolls' house, made
of wood covered
with lithographed
paper.

Schoenhut specialized in pretty bungalows with turned balustrades, net curtains and lithographed doorways showing a perspective view of the room beyond. They contained one to four rooms and a side opening. Models like these were produced until 1927.

Converse Toys and Woodenware Co. of Winchendon, Mass. also made lithographed paper-on-wood bungalows, with rather more primitive designs on them. Converse was founded by Morton E. Converse, who started business in about 1873. To entertain his sick daughter, he made her a dolls' tea table out of a box, and quickly realized that he had a saleable idea. The dolls' houses were small, simple bungalows with a verandah and printed windows and doors.

By 1890 Converse was the world's largest wood-toy manufacturer and Winchendon, was known as 'The Nuremberg of America'; yet by the 1930s this empire had disappeared.

The Stettheimer house

The Stettheimer house in the Museum of the City of New York was made by Carrie Stettheimer in 1923, out of wooden packing cases and furnished by her.

It depicts the lifestyle of a wealthy, cultured family of that time. There is a library-cum-games room, with Chinese lanterns, furniture and books, a brightly papered nursery with its own dolls' house, a master bedroom with green gilded furniture and pink walls, a butler's pantry, servants' rooms, a dining room, parlour, children's rooms and an art room containing miniature paintings by well-known American artists of the 1920s.

Colleen Moore's Castle

The actress Colleen Moore had seven dolls' houses, through her childhood and she began to collect miniatures. In 1928 when she was a movie star, she had a fairy castle built, designed and lighted by Hollywood set-designers and lighting experts, and decorated with themes from children's fairy tales, to house these.

The castle, now in the Museum of Science and Industry in Chicago, measures over 2.7m (9ft) square. It has electricity and plumbing systems, with running water in the bathrooms and kitchen.

When asked what period furniture he had used in the castle, Harold Grieve, the decorator, replied 'Early Fairy', and certainly the castle depicts the fantasy world of the 1930s with a rich mixture of myth, legend, fairy tale and Hollywood glitz.

buffet shows a collection of gold teapots, an ivory chocolate set and a breakfast set of china. Tapestries telling the life story of Sir Galahad hang on the walls. The bedroom of the Princess has a mother-of-pearl floor with a border of gold, and a canopied bed shaped like a fairy boat with a golden spider's-web coverlet.

BELOW The library of Colleen Moore's castle has tall, vaulted ceilings and tiny books, some of which contain hand written entries by famous authors.

LEFT The Museum of Science and Industry, Chicago is the home of Colleen Moore's castle. The castle has its own electricity and plumbing.

The entrance hall is hung with paintings of story-book characters, from Alice in Wonderland to Snow White, and a portrait of Colleen Moore. Cinderella's glass slippers were made by a skilled artisan from Michigan and, on a carved ivory table is a tiny pistol that shoots real silver bullets. The crowns of the Prince and Princess rest on a silver table, and near the crowns is a fairy wand with a diamond in its star. Etched glass windows the garden tell the stories of Jack and the Beanstalk, Prince Charming, and the Princess and the Seven Swans.

Colleen Moore's personal jewels were used to make some fittings. The drawing room has a floor made of rose quartz with a border of green jade and is lit by a diamond, emerald and pearl chandelier. A gold clock set with diamonds and emeralds is wound daily. The furniture is silver, except for the grand piano, which is made of rosewood with ivory legs.

King Arthur's dining hall has a round table set with a gold service, the forks marked with a monogram and each place is set with a goblet, plate and wine glasses. A

COLLECTING TWENTIETH CENTURY DOLLS' HOUSES

Dolls' houses made between the 1930s and 1950s offer good opportunities for collectors. Look out for the houses made by Lines, the market leader at the time. This firm produced many styles of dolls' house, most of which can be identified from old catalogues, varying from flat-fronted, plain-looking houses to quite elaborate models with balconies and porches. After World War I, three of the sons of the company's founder, Joseph Lines, set up as Triangtois. (The name was later abbreviated to Tri-ang) It was they who produced the 'Stockbroker Tudor' houses.

BELOW Tri-ang produced this typical 1932 Tudor stockbroker house, called the Gables. It is furnished with the commercially available furniture produced at the time and it was packed away before World War II.

English dolls' houses

In England, early-twentieth century dolls' houses made by craftsmen were still firmly rooted in the past, their exteriors resembling those of many substantial late Victorian villas.

There were plenty of commercially made dolls' houses available on the market for children whose parents could not afford the luxury of a hand-made model. Lithographed houses were being imported from America and also from France and Germany, but at the same time English toy firms were developing their own very individual style.

G & J Lines were rocking-horse makers in the 1880s and the first mention of a dolls' house produced by them was in 1898. By the early years of the twentieth century they were producing many different houses, from flat-fronted town houses to elaborate models with balconies and porches. One such, in the Lines catalogue of 1909–10, is described as: 'a really splendid mansion, elaborately fitted up, inside and out. Staircase, doors to rooms, French window, curtains, beautiful papers on the walls etc. 33in high 32in wide, price 75s'.

After World War I, three of the sons of Joseph Lines set up on their own, using the name Triangtois, which was later abbreviated to Tri-ang. As can be seen from a page of their coloured 1925–26 catalogue, they produced a wide range of attractive dolls' houses, some with balconies, others with shutters.

Late in the 1920s, Tri-ang started to make their Stockbroker Tudor houses, reflecting the current architectural fashion which still has reverberations in towns all over England. Tri-ang produced these dolls' houses right up until 1953. Valerie Ripley's 1932 house is a perfect example of a house of this kind, though there were many similar ones made in slightly different designs, all with Tudor beams and metal windows.

LEFT A 1930s English house with many home-made items of furniture.

The house is furnished with most of the well known brands of furniture of that time: Tri-ang, Pit-a-Pat, Taylor & Barrett and Tootsie Toy, as well as home-made items. They are all in perfect condition, because the house and its contents were packed away in a box before World War II where it remained unseen until its rediscovery in 1979.

In the dining room, the chairs, occasional table, fire-screen and stool are by Tri-ang, the canteen of cutlery by Pit-a-Pat and the dining table and desk are hand-made. The room is full of realistic details, such as the corkscrew and a metal bottle opener on the drinks table, a toast rack and salt shaker on the dining table and a sepia postcard on the desk. It is a charming evocation of middle-class life of the Thirties.

BELOW The dolls' house at Michelham Priory, England has a kitchen filled with all kinds of food.

The dolls' house at Michelham Priory, England, is a well-furnished house containing many of the commercially made pieces of furniture which were available during the 1920s. It was put together at this time by Mrs Turner, who eventually left it to the town. The dolls' house once had a front but this is not on view.

In the kitchen there is a miniature bottle of Enos fruit salts and there is a tiny gramophone with a record. In the nursery a miniature room which bears a striking resemblance to the one in the nursery of the Queen Mary house, as does the carved wooden soldier on his horse to some of the wooden toys in the royal nursery. The top floor bathroom contains everything a bath-room should have, including a medicine chest,

LEFT AND
BELOW This dolls'
house was made
for Mary Drewe
by her father. It
was designed by
the famous
architect Edwin
Lutyens.

The maid is seen laying the table in the dining room on the ground floor. There are napkins in rings, fish, salami and bread on the side table, glasses, jugs, knives, forks and spoons and a glass-fronted cupboard filled with cups, jugs and bowls. The table and chairs are part of the Triangtois Jacobean dining room suite, which dates it to before 1931.

The lady of the house has left the hall, with its luggage, wall phone, gong, grandfather clock, hat stand and fire extinguisher, and can be seen on her way to check how things are coming along in the kitchen. Although there is plenty of food about, a certain amount of disorder reigns. The maid is sitting down, there is no sign of a cook, and food is on the floor not far away from where two ivory mice are playing in front of a mousetrap.

A nanny's or maid's room has the basic furniture needed for servants' quarters, such as bed, radio, electric fire and wardrobe, and the laundry room is fully equipped with iron, a cupboard full of brooms, laundry basket, sewing machine and mangle.

The bedroom is so full of furniture (some of it by Triang) that it is almost impossible to see the bed, tucked away in the corner.

The middle floor has a sitting room, with a chess table and an ivory spinning wheel. On the grand piano there is a sheet of Dol-toi tunes. There are cakes on a tiered cakestand, a copy of The Times, Country Life and Tatler and a desk with scissors, pen, candlestick and flowers.

The father of the household is standing by the door. In the nursery on the other side of the landing one baby is perched in a highchair and another is lying in a cot.

A ROYAL HOBBY

Royalty all over the world has often taken a great interest in miniatures: Duke Albrecht of Germany, for example, had a wonderful house with a courtyard made for his daughter, which was destroyed by fire in 1674. There are also records that royal children were given miniatures to play with.

ABOVE Queen Mary's model of a room at Windsor Castle can be seen at the Bethnal Green Museum, London, England.

A seventeenth century cabinet house at the University of Uppsala in Sweden, made by the artist Philip Hainhofer, was said to have been bought by the town for presentation to King Gustavus Adolphus II of Sweden. The same artist made a house for Duke Philip of Pomerania.

In Denmark there is a famous dolls' house known as the Three Sisters House in the Dansk Folkemuseum, Copenhagen, which dates from about 1850. This house has a royal cipher of Crown Prince Frederick VIII of Denmark on the left side. The dolls' house was kept in the Yellow Palace, where Christian IX lived before he was created King in 1863 and it is thought that it was played with in the 1880s by Princess Alexandra (later Queen of England) and her sisters, Dagmar and Thyra.

English Queens

Queen Victoria had a dolls' house as a child. It is an ordinary little flat fronted house with a large front door flanked by two long, glazed windows and a smart fanlight above. It has two rooms furnished with the English and imported German furniture, but it has more than likely lost much of its original furniture.

Queen Mary of England had a quite ordinary house as a child. It is still arranged as it was when she was a child. There are six rooms, full of commercially made furniture. Queen Mary never lost her interest in dolls' houses. Mary's Windsor room, is a model of one in Windsor Castle. It has imitation lacquer furniture and painted curtains. In the same museum is Queen Mary's house, which was made in 1887. She bought it and supervised the furnishing.

She also had a cabinet containing two rooms made by David Allan, who was responsible for the upholstery and textiles at Buckingham Palace. The Queen collected the furniture and all the other items, herself. A Triangtois

catalogue for 1925–26 describes 'The Queen's dolls' House', (registered design 975508) as 'an exact reproduction of the design made famous by Her Majesty the Queen, who furnished the first model and gave it to the London Hospital for sale to raise funds.

The dolls' house for which Queen Mary is most famous, is the one now on permanent exhibition at Windsor Castle. This elaborate mansion was presented to the Queen and it was first shown to the public at the British Empire Exhibition at Wembley in 1924.

The mansion depicts a court residence of the early twentieth century in fine detail. The building was designed by the architect Sir Edwin Lutyens. It included every modern convenience, with electric lights and piped hot and cold water. The famous gardener Gertrude Jekyll planned the garden, which is contained in a drawer, the trees lie flat when the drawer is closed. The lawns are green velvet, flower beds are planted with summer flowers made of metal, climbing roses trail over the walls, and the garden even contains miniature snails and butterflies.

In 1932, Princess Elizabeth was presented with a thatched Wendy house by the people of Wales. Tri-ang were not slow to leap on the bandwagon and in 1939 there appeared in their catalogue. The Princess dolls' House, 'a model of the dolls' house presented to Princess Elizabeth by the Welsh people'. It was double fronted with four rooms, a hall, staircase and landing. It had opening metal windows, imitation thatched roof and electric lights. The front was hinged.

There was also a larger model with four rooms, five electric lights, a bathroom with dummy bath, a kitchen with a dummy sink and gas stove, and a garage with opening doors.

ABOVE Princess Elizabeth and her sister Margaret playing in the house given to them by the people of Wales in 1932.

LEFT The dolls' house version of the Welsh house given to the Princess, produced by the Tri-ang company.

RIGHT The
impressive
carpeted hallway
of Pembroke
Palace.

ABOVE The double-cube room of Sir
Nevile Wilkinson's dolls' house Pembroke
Palace contains portraits of his father-in-
law, his daughter Gwendoline and a self
portrait. Other paintings are copies of
paintings in Wilton House.

of stuffed furniture and a little glass-fronted cupboard, a table and a piano, all typical of their period. There are two bedrooms, one simply furnished with an iron bed, the other grander, with a brass bed hung about with elaborate curtains. On the ground floor, there is a large central hall with a staircase rising from it, a dining room and the unusual addition of a schoolroom. Two children are sitting at a set of desks in front of the teacher, who has her own desk. The rooms at the back presumably include a kitchen, bathroom and servants' quarters.

Castle Drogo

Some dolls' houses of the 1920s have interesting con-nections. At Castle Drogo, near Exeter, Devon, which was designed by the famous architect Edwin Lutyens for Julius Drewe, the successful founder of the Home and Colonial stores, is a 1.52m (5ft) high dolls' house which resembles a Lutyens country house.

The Castle was begun in 1910 and completed in 1930, but the dolls' house, which was built for Mr Drewe's daughter Mary, has its date, 1906, clearly written on its front, with Mary's initials in the middle. Little is known about the house apart from the fact that it was made for her by a carpenter at Wadhurst.

The front and back wind down into the base at the turn of a handle but because of its position, only one side of the house is on view. We can see into the panelled drawing room on the first floor, which has a good suite

BELOW The
dining room of
Pembroke Palace
has a frieze on
the ceiling by
Bobbie Simmons.

The Dining room

Pembroke Palace

Sir Nevile Wilkinson, a British soldier-artist, made a miniature mansion known as Pembroke Palace, which was 'opened' by Queen Alexandra in 1908 and is now permanently exhibited at Wilton House in Wiltshire. It is 2.1m (6ft) long and 1.25m (4ft) high, on three floors. The main hall, the dining room and the double-cube room, although restored, are Sir Nevile's original work. Three of his paintings hang in the double-cube room.

ABOVE Titania's palace stands on a platform at Legoland so that it can be viewed from all sides.

Titania's Palace

Perhaps the most splendid dolls' house of all time, Titania's Palace, was conceived by Sir Nevile in 1907. He was sketching a tree near his home in Ireland when his small daughter said that she had seen a fairy disappearing into the tree. He decided that the fairy was none other than Titania, Queen of the Fairies, and offered to build a palace for her and her husband, Oberon.

It is a palace in miniature, built round a courtyard laid out as a garden and designed to be viewed from all sides. It is in eight sections, each with a removable front, so that it can fit into a packing case. It is now in the museum at Legoland, Copenhagen. The style of the architecture is varied, with Greek influence in the columns, English in the windows and Italian in the Palladian frieze and in the state apartments.

A great deal of time and care has been lavished on the state apartments. One of them, the Hall of the Fairy Kiss, is the formal entrance to the palace. It has a minstrel gallery ornamented with silver and bronze figures and a glass casket containing the insignia of the Fairy Kiss, the highest order of Fairyland.

The palace is full of whimsical touches, like the silver grilles designed to keep the junior fairies from flying into the hall. There is no kitchen, because fairies do not need food; the dining-room table is set with a glass dinner service but no knives or forks; cupboards for the storage of spare wings are provided in the princesses' bedroom; the baths have no drains or taps because fairies bathe in dewdrops. None of the doors have handles or locks, because fairy doors open by themselves.

Titania's Palace was nearing completion when Sir Nevile heard rumours of the building of Queen Mary's dolls' house. He feared that this splendid creation would overshadow his own and he hurried to try to complete his palace, but in the end he had to present it unfinished at an exhibition in 1922.

*LEFT The Hall of
the Guilds, Titania's
Palace. The floor is
black and white
marble and is
decorated with
flags and fairy
paintings.*

MIRROR GRANGE

In England in the 1920s and 1930s, there was a popular strip cartoon in the newspaper *The Daily Mirror* recounting the adventures of an unlikely trio of animals, a penguin, a dog and a rabbit, named Pip, Squeak and Wilfred. These imaginary creatures had a miniature house built for them. It was described as 'a house in miniature, a home (but of no ordinary design), with cosy rooms and fascinating furniture, of cunningly contrived vistas and charming nooks with an imposing tower'.

The house was designed by Maxwell Ayrton, joint architect of the Wembley Exhibition, and it was built in 1929.

Famous artists like Sir William, Orpen painted portraits to decorate the walls. Mirror Grange, as it was called, made its first public appearance at the Grafton Galleries, the small charge for admission going to the Heritage Craft Schools for Crippled Children at Chailey, which was its last resting place.

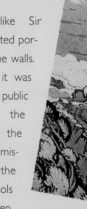

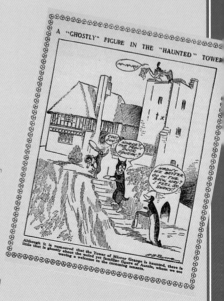

ABOVE RIGHT This painting by Victor Hembrow of Mirror Grange is taken from a book written about it and published by the newspaper.

RIGHT The characters from the cartoon strip are shown here on their way to the house. Auntie can be seen waving from the top of the tower.

LEFT The house on the rock — Mirror Grange— has models of the animals walking up the stairs. The tower opens and furniture can be stored in the rock.

CHAPTER FIVE

CREATING MINIATURES

• • • •

Making your own dolls' house or furnishings can be the most rewarding part of collecting dolls' houses or dolls' house furniture. Today many makers specialize in creating $\frac{1}{12}$-scale pieces based on nineteenth century designs, while miniature wallpaper, mouldings and building supplies are all readily available through mail order, shows and miniature stores. Whichever style you select, good references are essential for it is accuracy that is a major factor in creating a successful miniature.

But before beginning a project, select a specific date. Then choose the location with an idea of who would be the house's imaginary inhabitants. Make sure that the exterior of the house matches the interior decorations.

Work materials

A few basic tools will be needed: sandpaper, in fine and medium grades, for use on walls and furniture alike; a sharp craft knife for cutting wallpaper and trimming kits; a measuring rule; a metal straight edge and a pencil. For slightly more advanced work, you may also need: a modeller's saw and mitre block; a small drill; and perhaps a jigsaw for cutting doorways, fireplaces and windows.

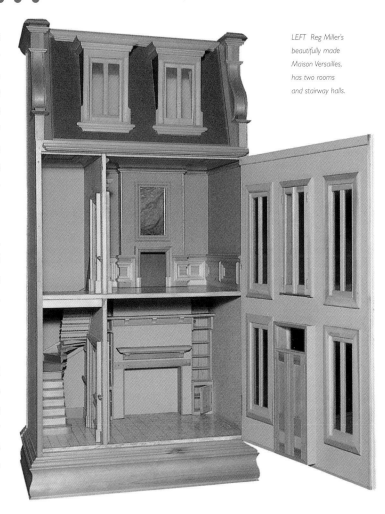

LEFT Reg Miller's beautifully made Maison Versailles, has two rooms and stairway halls.

RIGHT The kitchen of Caroline Hamilton's thirteen room house which she made and furnished herself.

BELOW The bathroom of Joan Gibson's cabinet house is stocked with all the items needed for the inhabitants to make their ablutions.

Finally, for decoration, small paintbrushes and artist's brushes are needed for paint work and wood-staining, crack filler for uneven corners or discrepancies in the woodwork, wood glue and a pot of wallpaper paste.

The room settings shown in this book will provide a guide to varying styles and a source of inspiration for creating dolls' house miniatures.

Miniature makers

Reg Miller is an English craftsman working in wood in the best tradition of the eighteenth century. His houses are beautifully constructed, in wood on an inch-to-a-foot ($\frac{1}{12}$) scale. Each house is based on a real house and he researches his subject meticulously.

Italian-born Bernardo Traettino is a fine craftsman who started by making some miniature furniture as a Christmas gift for a child he knew. He produces bespoke products directly for customers and has made houses in every possible style from Tudor to modern, using traditional materials.

Caroline Hamilton is a dolls'-house enthusiast. From homes created for her dolls in shoe boxes, she graduated to proper dolls' houses. She also refurnishes old dolls' houses.

Retired teacher Joan Gibson has a collection of several dolls' houses and is an accomplished miniature maker and collector. Joan Gibson's houses have their own inhabitants, each of them with their own character.